UNDERSTANDING

Martina E. Faulkner MSW

Foreword by
Kate Lund PhD

INSPIREBYTES OMNI MEDIA

This publication is published and distributed worldwide in the English language in the following formats:

ISBN Hardcover: 978-1-969348-04-4
ISBN Paperback: 978-1-969348-05-1
ISBN E-Book: 978-1-969348-06-8
Library of Congress Control Number: 2025945666

This book was printed in a manner that minimizes its impact on the planet and the environment. Learn more at: www.inspirebytes.com/why-we-publish-differently/

 INSPIREBYTES OMNI MEDIA

Inspirebytes Omni Media LLC
PO Box 988
Wilmette, IL 60091

For more information, please visit www.inspirebytes.com.

Human Authored™, Reg #: 6482419
Learn more about the Human Authored initiative at authorsguild.org/human

For Lucas

Contents

Contents

Foreword by Dr. Kate Lund

In a world that often prioritizes quick fixes, instant gratification, and surface-level solutions, *The Understanding Series* by Martina Faulkner offers a refreshing and much-needed alternative: A path inward. With depth, clarity, and compassion, Martina invites us to pause, reflect, and engage more intentionally with the foundational truths that shape our lives. In doing so, she opens the door to a deeper, more connected way of being.

Across the series—which focuses on *Resilience, Grief, Compassion, Energy, Gratitude,* and *Karma*—Martina explores some of the most vital themes of the human experience. Each subject stands firmly on its own, yet when read together, they create a tapestry of insight that is both richly layered and deeply cohesive. The series isn't about offering neat answers or telling readers what to think; instead, it gently challenges us to become more curious, more present, and more open to the complexity and beauty of our personal journeys.

Martina's voice is uniquely powerful. She brings together spiritual insight, lived experience, and a grounded perspective that feels both expansive and deeply relatable. Her writing is not just thoughtful, it's human. She doesn't speak from a pedestal; she walks alongside us, offering questions, perspectives, and reflections that illuminate a path towards a deeper understanding of our own human experience. Through her work, we're reminded that true understanding doesn't come from judgment or control; it comes from compassion, from allowing, and from the willingness to sit with discomfort long enough to learn from it.

As a clinical psychologist who has spent much of my career exploring resilience, emotional intelligence, and the power of mindset, I found myself resonating with the themes throughout this series on a personal and professional level. I had the pleasure of exploring each of these topics with Martina in conversation on my podcast, *The Optimized Mind*. Those discussions, like her writing, were rich, vulnerable, and expansive. Martina has a gift for holding space and asking the questions that matter. She helps us see what's often hidden beneath the surface, and she does so with deep empathy and grace.

Whether you are navigating the complexities of grief, seeking to cultivate more gratitude in your daily life, trying to tap into a deeper well of resilience, or simply hoping to reconnect with your sense of purpose, *UNDERSTANDING* offers tools and insights to do just this. It meets you where you are, without judgment, and encourages you to trust the unfolding process of your own experience in a way which allows you to thrive within your own unique context.

In an age where so many of us are searching for meaning, connection, and clarity, this series is a powerful offering. It is both timeless and timely. I believe that each reader will find something unique and personal in these pages; something that speaks directly to their own experience and helps them move forward with more awareness and intention.

Dr. Kate Lund

Clinical Psychologist, Author and Host of
The Optimized Mind Podcast

Introduction

When I first set out to write this series, it wasn't a series—it was a single book. Actually, it wasn't even a book. The original idea was to write an essay on karma that was longer than a blog and focused more on theory than application. Why? Well, here's the story:

In August 2018, I wrote a blog titled *The Law of Karma and Wishing Harm on Others.* At the time, people in my life (both personal and professional) were asking me whether it was ever okay to wish harm on someone. They asked so frequently that I thought others might also benefit from my perspective on the subject, so I wrote a blog. It started like this:

> *When is it ok to wish ill on someone?*
>
> *Well, the short answer is: never.*
>
> *And the long answer is: Really, NEVER.*
>
> *It's never ok to wish harm on anyone else. If you do, you're actually inviting that bad energy back into your life tenfold. Karma doesn't discriminate in that regard —what you reap, you will (eventually) sow. Always.*

Even though I had an inkling that my words might help, I could never have expected the response that followed. Over the course of the next six years, the blog grew and generated millions of search impressions and thousands of new monthly readers on a consistent basis (and is still going strong as of writing this book). It also prompted lots of comments from people who wanted to ask questions about their own situations. And, though I tried to respond to as many as I could (especially if someone was hurting), it quickly became unsustainable and I had to turn commenting off.

What did this type of response tell me? Well, my "web guy" told me that companies pay a lot of money to get that kind of traffic. Yet, to me, this was just a blog explaining a larger concept in simple, easy-to-understand terms. So, what was *really* going on? When I looked more closely at the analytics, I realized what was happening and it was somewhat startling. The most commonly searched phrases that resulted in people landing on my blog looked something like this:

- "Wishing ill on someone karma"
- "What happens if you wish death on someone"
- "Wishing bad karma on someone"

Now, I am genuinely glad that Google decided to put forward my blog that said to "never do it" instead of someone else's blog that taught you *how* to do it. For that, I am grateful. But the analytics told me something much deeper and more important: People were hurting.

In fact, the fact that the numbers have only increased over the years tells me that lots and lots of people *are* hurting.

It takes a lot of pain (or fear) to wish harm on someone. And the fact that they wanted to learn more about the relationship between inflicting harm on someone and their own karma tells me that they already knew that it wasn't a good idea before they started typing in the words. To me, their searching for this type of information meant that they still felt wishing harm was worth it on some level, even if it affected their karma. In other words, they were hurting so much that it didn't matter if they got hurt some more, as long as they could also hurt the person who was hurting them.

This broke my heart.

As I already mentioned, I tried to respond whenever I could, knowing that I couldn't help everyone. Eventually, a colleague suggested that I write a longer piece to try and help more people, but I was too busy to add this to my list for a while. Then, something else happened: In 2024, I watched the search numbers rise. By January 2025, I knew it was time to *make* time.

When I finally sat down to write, I found that I had a lot more to say than an essay could accommodate and *Understanding Karma* was born. At the time, I also decided to make it a visual experience, because of the nature of karma itself. I wanted to create a simple book that was easily accessible and would help people heal as they turned its pages. As a Reiki Master Teacher, I know the power of words as well as the power of images.

Blending the two felt appropriate as I married language with colors and imagery to create something truly unique and inherently healing.

So, How Did the Series Come About?

During one of my meditations while I was finishing *Understanding Karma*, I asked the universe how I could better serve and the answer was clear and brief: "Create and Build." I looked at the book I had created and realized that I had a template for something bigger. I realized that I could use *Understanding Karma* as a launching pad for a series that addressed other commonly-asked questions or topics.

For almost two decades, I have helped others using various modalities that bridge the mind-body-soul frontier. I have earned a trifecta in helping degrees and certifications, which puts me in a unique position to synthesize multiple teachings—making them effective and applicable to almost everyone and anyone. Being a helping professional means that I often hear the same questions from different people, regardless of their situation. With the template I created for the first book, I could now address some of the topics I have been asked about the most over the years.

So, when I sat down to make a list of topics for the series, I reflected on 20+ years of client queries. I thought about what I have been asked to clarify the most during this timeframe—the most misunderstood concepts—and I came up with five areas to focus on: Grief, Gratitude, Resilience, Energy, and Hope.[1] I was satisfied with this list, but a trusted friend suggested I add a sixth: Compassion.

With these six topics (including Karma), the series was set and all I had to do was write. Drawing on my years of experience, I sat down and got to work.

One of the things I have repeatedly come across in my time as a helping professional is a significant amount of confusion over

---

[1] Hope was part of the original list, but since I was already writing a full-length book on this topic, I decided to remove it from the series.

some of the basics. These are foundational pieces that can truly impact a person's ability to apply healthy solutions to more complex issues. For example, if you don't understand the underlying reason for grief and why grieving is important, it can be harder to navigate when someone dies. This can keep you feeling stuck, because it's more challenging for you to access the helping words of others since the core concept is still out of reach.

Therefore, I've looked at these topics with a much broader view—one that provides a basic explanation that is universal. In this way, my hope is to make each subject more accessible and easier to understand and incorporate in your life.

In my experience, when we take the time to see things from a higher perspective, we can apply solutions more easily. Understanding is what gives us access to application. It's for that reason that I've written this series and why I think it's important. I want to bring an easier understanding to things that we all experience as human beings, in a way that can help make solutions more accessible and applicable.

I think understanding is something we often overlook when helping people, or even moving through our own life. At some point, we are just expected to know things we were never taught, which can be tricky to navigate. Often, we feel embarrassed to ask the basics or even to request some clarity. My hope is that reading this book will help to provide a baseline for you—a place where you can start to ask more questions that specifically apply to you to help you find solutions for your particular situation.

Ultimately, *UNDERSTANDING* is meant to be of service. It's designed to inform and inspire and was written to help us all navigate life with greater ease. Regardless of which topic currently interests you most (or which topic you need most), each of the subjects can provide you with a deeper sense of self—of what it means to be human—as well as a deeper sense of the world around you.

A Note On How to Use This Book

As you've probably figured out already, I'm a firm believer in making sure that self-help books are not only accessible, but applicable. I also know that it's important to present things in a way that makes it easier to receive them. When I originally wrote the series, it was in a different order than it is presented in this book because standalone topics don't necessarily need to flow into one another. However, when it came time to compile them into one book, I needed to rethink the cadence of the topics while also adding a bit more narrative.

Writing in this way is kind of like making a mixtape (or playlist, for the younger reader). How each topic flows into the next sets an underlying tone for the book. The cadence I have created is deliberate; it's designed to take you on a journey as you move through each topic if you are reading the book straight through. However, if you need to start with a specific topic, then do that. Even though the book was designed to have a flow, how you use it is up to you. At the end of the day, what works for you is what matters most.

When we can acquire knowledge through understanding, life has the potential to become easier. My wish for you is that you find the words on these pages to be the vehicle that brings you more grace, ease, and inner peace.

UNDERSTANDING

RESILIENCE

"Like tiny seeds with potent power to push through tough ground and become mighty trees, we hold innate reserves of unimaginable strength. We are resilient."

Catherine DeVrye

Introduction

"When we learn how to become resilient, we learn how to embrace the beautifully broad spectrum of the human experience."

– Jaeda Dewalt

How do you define resilience? Some might say it's about strength, while others could argue that it's more about flexibility. We can identify it when we see it in others, and we also know what it feels like for ourselves. There are times when we can see resilience as a kind of softness in the midst of brutality, or as a firmness when things are poorly-defined or chaotic. Interestingly, we are also able to recognize when we see someone who isn't being resilient.

However, even with all this knowledge and understanding, it's still not always easy to clearly define resilience when someone asks you what it is. So, let's look at the Merriam-Webster dictionary, which gives us two definitions:

1. The capability of a strained body to recover its size and shape after deformation caused especially by compressive stress

2. An ability to recover from or adjust easily to misfortune or change

As humans, it's the second entry that matters. As stated, it's pretty easy to understand. So, why is it so hard for us to describe simply when we are asked? Even though resilience may be easy to recognize, it's challenging for us to truly define in application because it can be expressed in so many unique ways. We know it when we see it and often put it on a pedestal as something to strive toward. And yet, there is no specific or singular way to actually achieve it.

So, what is resilience, actually, and perhaps more importantly, how do we create it?

What Is Resilience?

"Resilience is knowing that you are the only one that has the power and the responsibility to pick yourself up. "

– Mary Holloway

Simply stated: Resilience is an outward expression of inner growth. It's a state of being that is the result of showing up repeatedly and consistently over time. When we show up for ourselves and actually do the work we need to do to grow and evolve, we build a few byproducts, one of which is resilience. This, in turn, allows us to find a core stability that we can draw on in both daily life and when things become challenging.

Resilience Is a Byproduct

As a byproduct of other endeavors, you can't set out with a specific goal to cultivate resilience. This means that when you make the decision to work on yourself in a way that supports your inner growth (mentally, emotionally, and spiritually), you are building resilience at the same time, but not because you set out to achieve resilience. In that regard, resilience is a positive side effect of making decisions to work on yourself and your soul's progression. In the same way that physically working out your body can create muscle memory alongside strength, working on your inner world can create resilience alongside the goal of healing.

So, if resilience is the outward expression of the inner work, this also means that it is the result of the soul working in conjunction with the body, mind, and emotions. Therefore, it's multi-faceted in how it can serve you as you continue to move forward through life. This is why it can show up in so many different ways, from strength to flexibility, from softness to firmness.

It's also why we can so easily identify it when we see it happening in front of us, and why we can call things out that are supposed to look like resilience, but aren't, such as when someone is showing off strength by overcompensating. In pop culture, we sometimes call it the "Napoleon complex" or the "B.M.O.C" (Big Man On Campus) trope. This display of "strength" is primarily posturing, which makes it performative; it's not, therefore, actual strength... or resilience.

Resilience Is Not a Shield

Furthermore, since strength is one of the ways we interpret or experience resilience, it can sometimes be used incorrectly in an attempt to be resilient. Unfortunately in these situations, what's really happening is anything but. Brute force is not resilience. True resilience is not a shield. To think that is a common mistake and one that needs to be redirected.

When someone puts emotional armor on to protect themselves from others, this is not a form of resilience; it's a response to fear. Since resilience is the result of doing inner work, true resilience comes from the inside, not the outside. Shields and armor are based in force, and force is often based in some measure of fear. Resilience, on the other hand, is rooted in truth, growth, and understanding.

To understand resilience is to know *who* you are as well as *why* you are.

Why do you show up for things, or not? What makes you feel more engaged, or more invested and passionate? Yes, it's true that resilience creates a form of protection, but it's not a layer on the outside that you need strength to uphold; it's a resource on the inside that requires no strength from you, only alignment.

Resilience, therefore, is both a state of mind and a state of being. It is a presence as well as knowledge. When you have done the work on emotional, mental, and spiritual levels, your mind is able to bring all those pieces together into the present moment in new ways.

If you then add a physical layer to it, you can truly stand in your boots and feel rooted in who you are in your presence. This also means that resilience is about being who you are and no longer feeling compelled to chase different definitions of yourself.

When you build resilience, you shift how you show up in life. You could say that resilience gives you a new user's manual to life. In that way, it is similar to the tools in your mental-emotional toolbox. However, because it's not something you can go out and acquire or achieve, it's not an actual tool (like breathwork, or meditation).

Acquiring resilience is a process and it takes time. It also takes consistency and a willingness to change. When you continually choose to show up for yourself, you will build resilience.

Doing Due Diligence

"Do not judge me by my success, judge me by how many times I fell down and got back up again."
– Nelson Mandela

Even though resilience is not something you can specifically set out to learn, there are things that you can learn—that you must learn, actually—in order to build resilience. Most importantly, you will need a mindset shift, but in order to achieve a shift in your thinking, you have to engage in some due diligence.

What Is Due Diligence?

Due diligence is most often associated with business and law, though it can be used as a tool by anyone. Simply stated, due diligence is a thorough and considerate approach to gathering appropriate information before making a decision. For example, if you are buying a house, you will want to learn more about the house itself and do an inspection, just as you will want to learn about the neighborhood and community. By researching and gathering this data, you will be able to make a better (stronger, healthier) decision. As a practice or mindset, due diligence can be incorporated in more personal capacities.

When it comes to building resilience, embracing due diligence is a necessary step. It's what allows your mind to shift from one that is externally-focused to one that is internally-aligned. Internal-alignment is not to be interpreted as being self-centered, egotistical, or narcissistic. Those are unhealthy approaches to life for the individual and everyone around them (and have nothing to do with resilience). An internally-aligned mind is about recon-necting to yourself in a way that allows you to truly get to know who you are, what makes you tick, and how you want to show up in the world.

As an example, this would be a shift from wanting to wear the latest fashion trend even though you genuinely don't like it (external focus), to one where you acknowledge the latest fashion trend exists, while still honoring your inner truth and not adopting it or choosing to make aspects of it your own (inner alignment). In other words, if you don't want to wear a belt bag (aka: bum bag, fanny pack) across your chest, you don't have to. Most importantly, when you engage in due diligence and this kind of alignment, you will feel good about your decision, because it came from inside you, rather than as an emotional reaction to something external. This is a form of resilience.

By connecting with who you are inside and reinforcing those bonds through inner work, you learn more about yourself. Due diligence is what provides you with the foundational footing you need to build resilience.

So, if you think resilience sort of just "happens"... it doesn't. Although it may be true that some people look back on their life and suddenly realize they are resilient, the change didn't happen overnight. Even though the realization that you are resilient may feel sudden, the actual work to create resilience always involves a measure of time and effort.

Empowerment vs. Power

"I can be changed by what happens to me. But I refuse to be reduced by it."

– Maya Angelou

In addition to requiring due diligence to shift your mindset, you also need to understand the difference between empowerment and power. This is similar to the previous section's focus on internal alignment and external focus, with an added perspective around intent and action.

When we talk about both power and empowerment, there is usually an unspoken aspect: Outcome. Typically, both power and empowerment have a desired outcome attached to them. This is the identified (and sometimes unidentified) intent behind the action.

When aligned with power, the desired outcome is often one that serves to reinforce the power, even if it does something else along the way. Interestingly, the same can be said about empowerment: Empowerment's desired outcome is to generate more empowerment. There is, however, a major difference between the two beyond just their impact, which is also notable. That difference is their fuel requirement.

Unlike empowerment, power requires a constant fuel source. It must always be fed in order to stay relevant. Empowerment, on the other hand, continues to exist once it is created. Even though acts of empowerment may serve to reinforce it, if there are no future acts of empowerment, it still remains intact. The same cannot be said for power. Power, as a construct, is fleeting and requires constant maintenance through reinforcement.

For examples of this, we can look at the greatest use of power in the world: dictatorships and authoritarian regimes. They continually need to engage in power struggles in order to exert their power and prove they still have it. In fact, they often *create* power struggles just for this purpose. This means that power is an externally-focused initiative. It must always look outside itself in order to exist. It has to have something to push against in order to feel true, to be considered valid or real.

Conversely, empowerment is internally-aligned. Once it has been created, it stays. It may go quiet or dormant for a while as circumstances change, but if you need it, it's there. You can always call on it once it's created. It never needs an ongoing fuel source, though it can be reinforced by engaging in more empowering actions. As such, empowerment is a bedfellow of resilience, whereas power is not.

Even though both empowerment and power can appear to be about strength, when it comes to resilience, only one is truly strong because it's lasting. And just like empowerment, resilience is lasting. Once you have created it, it's there. Always.

It can build on itself, but it never goes away. Not really. It may feel out of reach when situations change or are new, but it's still there, just waiting for you to remember and call on it.

Who Is Most Resilient?

"It's your reaction to adversity, not adversity itself that determines how your life's story will develop."
– Dieter F. Uchtdorf

Everyone has some measure of resilience within them. As children, we are taught how to stumble, fall, and try again. This is how most infants turn into toddlers (and why we call them toddlers—because they toddle). To toddle is to take short unsteady steps while learning to walk. The key word in all of that is: Learning.

Learning builds resilience.

Yes, it really is that simple. As long as you are open to learning, you can build resilience. This also means that everybody is resilient on some level. So, who is most resilient? Before we dive into that, we need to start with a bit of a qualifier.

Don't Put People on Pedestals

In our aspirational culture, we have a tendency to put people on pedestals. We do this because they have something we want—or think we want (because we're told we should want it). These individuals have something we think we can't have, something that often feels out of reach or unattainable.

This is what makes it aspirational. When something feels aspirational, our response is often to put that person (and/or the quality) on a pedestal—forever keeping it out of reach and above us. But it bears noting that *we* are the ones doing that. Even if someone wants to be on a pedestal in relation to our lives, only *we* can actually put them there. If we choose not to see them on a pedestal, they aren't.

The same applies for qualities that people display. If, for example, you put resilience on a pedestal, you are the one that is making it aspirational. Your idealization of their resilience is what makes it seem out of reach, not the resilient person's behavior or presence.

Therefore, in order to talk about the people who are most resilient, we must first understand that nobody is on a pedestal, nor should they be. Their life is different (not better or worse) than others' lives, and as a result, they have built more resilience.

Resilient People

In general, the people who are most resilient are the ones that have been willing to show up at their most vulnerable and have been humble enough to learn. They have been curious enough to engage with life in a different way and have been open enough to accept wisdom from others. The people who are most resilient are those that have made a choice to become the best versions of themselves. Simultaneously, they also understand that the best version is always part of a process of evolution and growth—and always a continual work in progress.

For some, this process can take a lot of time and involve a fair amount of hardship and struggle. For others, it can seem easier or smoother, involving less struggle, but with some challenges. For both, it always includes a measure of humility, curiosity, and willingness.

Conversely, for example, if you are unable to be humble and curious (you often or always think you're "right"), you will not build resilience. Similarly, if you are looking to blame others and you are not willing to engage differently, you will not build resilience. Resilience is a byproduct of growth, and as such, it requires you to check your ego at the door so that you can actually learn and evolve.

The most resilient among us have learned this—often the hard way.

When someone says "I want to be like you" to someone who is very resilient, it's highly likely that the resilient person is saying in their head, "be careful what you wish for" because they know that their resilience was hard-won.

We are all, always, in a state of becoming. Who you choose to become is up to you. How you choose to engage is up to you.

A more resilient person understands this and focuses on both the long-game and the present at the same time. They know that life is much more than just this moment, and simultaneously, they know the importance of how they show up in the present moment. In other words, nobody suddenly becomes the best version of themselves. Nor is a "best version" something to be achieved like a milestone, where it's "one and done." It's always an on-going process.

The more accurate phrase would be: To be the best version of yourself, now. Today. In this moment. This approach means that you have left room for an even better version of yourself in the next moment. A resilient person understands that they are always growing, while still enjoying who they have become and appreciating all the work they have already done to get there.

A person who desires to be resilient, and isn't willing to do the work, will end up in a constant cycle of chasing resilience, which ultimately undermines any resilience they may have already had, making it the one way resilience can actually fade or fail.

Chasing Resilience Is a Resilience-Killer

Chasing resilience chips away at whatever resilience is already there, because it goes against the truth that it's a byproduct of other work. By making resilience the focused goal (which is externally-driven), you are actually redefining what resilience is and thereby removing any resilience you had by reclassifying it. This means that your existing resilience is undermined by your pursuit of more resilience as a goal.

Resilience needs to be an internal process and there is nobody whose life you can compare to your own to then be able to go and learn their lessons and become resilient yourself. You have to do it based on your own life, your own life experiences, your own mind, your own heart, your own body, and your own soul. It cannot be done by adopting somebody else's work, tools, experience, or exercises.

When Do We Need Resilience Most?

"Life doesn't get easier or more forgiving, we get stronger and more resilient."

– Steve Maraboli

Though it may seem counterintuitive, we need resilience most in our daily life. A lot of people think that we need resilience the most when we are in crisis, but that's not true. In a crisis, we can draw on other resources (including resilience) to help us get through. In daily life, resilience is one of our primary tools, if not the primary tool we use. We just rarely name it that.

Think about it this way: In your everyday life, there are certain things you do that are both for the present moment as well as the long run. For example, brushing your teeth is something that serves you now (your teeth are clean and your mouth and breath are fresh), and later (you prevent cavities and other issues). Brushing your teeth is like building resilience; it serves you both today and in the long-run. It works when you are consistent over time, as well as flexible in how you allow it to evolve. (Most of us have changed the way we brush our teeth from when we were children, for example, by both necessity and preference.)

This flexibility is what makes resilience so important in our daily lives. It is what allows us to navigate annoying situations with more ease, staying grounded in who we are. This looks like the person in line at the store who seems to be unfazed by the cashier chatting with the other customers in front of them. In truth, unless you are a first responder and there is an emergency, there is no reason to get frustrated by someone taking an extra 15–30 seconds to enjoy a conversation. Even if it's a minute, it's still not going to really impact anybody's day in a negative way; however, it might improve both the cashier and the customer's day immensely. A more resilient person knows this. They choose to remain calm and happy in themselves while waiting in line.

Conversely, a less resilient person might get more frustrated, start to complain, and try to engage people around them to join in with their complaint. This is because when someone isn't feeling resilient, they move from a place of empowerment to a place of seeking power, and power needs fuel. By engaging other people in the complaint, the less resilient person has acquired the fuel he or she needs to continue to complain, and the cycle continues. This keeps the person out of opportunity for growth and out of opportunity for building resilience.

This is why we need more resilience in our daily lives than when we are in crisis, tragedy, or trauma. The truth of the matter is that it's the daily struggles we encounter as humans that wear us down and erode our will and well-being over time. By necessity, resilience really comes into play when you are navigating life's daily obstacles that serve to undermine the higher frequency emotions of hope, love, joy, or peace.

What are "high-frequency emotions"?
These are the emotions that we consider to be on the higher end of the "positive-negative" spectrum. Instead of labeling them "good" or "bad" (as no emotion has such inherent value), it's more accurate to say high- or low-frequency. In other words, when they vibe higher on the spectrum, they feel lighter, making us feel better.

When it comes to resilience, it's best and most often used in daily life. It helps us make our daily existence easier and better. It also helps to create more opportunities for us to experience higher frequency emotions. Resilience is required to maintain some measure of inner peace. It is required to maintain a belief in hope, love, and joy. Therefore, we need resilience the most on a daily basis.

What About Trauma And Tragedy?

"Resilience is based on compassion for ourselves as well as compassion for others."

– Sharon Salzberg

Though resilience is part of the equation, crises will always require a layer of strength that we don't regularly access in our daily life—and shouldn't need to. These circumstances are most often born of something extreme or egregious, such as trauma or tragedy. If these are part of your daily life, then that is a totally different situation than what we are discussing with regard to resilience. (In instances where trauma and tragedy are part of daily life, we are talking about a different type of strength—one that includes fortitude and tenacity and is more about survival than resilience.)

Now, when it comes to an unexpected crisis, you rarely get through it by being resilient alone. In other words, resilience by itself is not enough to get through a tragedy or trauma. Instead, most people initially get through those situations by drawing on other resources. For example, they may have an adrenaline rush that helps them focus and manage the situation well enough to get to a place where the crisis can abate and things can "normalize." Then, once a new normal is created, resilience is back at the helm helping the person create new ways to navigate daily life.

Though trauma and tragedy will draw on some measure of strength and flexibility (which we often understand to be a form of resilience), they often require other short-term resources to get through the intensity of the situation. Once the intense period is over, that is when resilience takes center stage again, helping us to (re)adjust to daily life and create stability.

Resilience And Choice

"Persistence and resilience only come from having been given the chance to work through difficult problems."
– Gever Tulley

As we have already discussed, resilience is not something you can obtain in a book, a meditation, or a yoga class. Nor is it something you can acquire by listening to others, such as in podcasts or webinars. Resilience is—and always will be—an inside job.

That being said, it is possible to learn about resilience (what it means and what it might feel like) by reading a book or listening to someone's story. This can help you better recognize it when you are undergoing it or experiencing it, which can then help you make decisions that reinforce it. But, in order to truly grow your own resilience, it has to be done in the day-to-day things that help support you in your well-being and on your soul's path and journey.

What are these things? They are the daily decisions you make in your life that offer you opportunities to shift your thinking and your perspective. This is how you build resilience: Through choice.

To use an earlier example: Consider your most mundane activities, such as grocery shopping. Now, think about the last time you were frustrated because something was happening outside your control. In that moment—that very real, very simple moment—you had a choice. You could either get frustrated and ramp up your low frequency emotions, or you could take a breath and choose to occupy your mind in a different, healthier way.

Which did you choose? And what was the result?

If you chose to ramp up, what could you do differently next time to make a different choice? If you chose to occupy your mind, what other ways could you occupy your mind that feel even more aligned with your well-being? (Could you read a funny text or meme instead of checking work emails, for example?)

Building resilience is all about the little choices we make on a daily basis and how we learn from them. If you're not willing to learn, you can't gain resilience. More importantly, perhaps, if you don't see those small events as opportunities to learn, you will be making this much harder than it needs to be.

Now, if you can't see these opportunities through the lens of learning, how about seeing them as something else? It's true that sometimes we don't want to see something as a learning opportunity because it triggers us. When we feel triggered, most opportunities are off the table. But there's another way... remembering.

Remembering is a tool you can use to take some of the triggers out of a situation that is "pinging" you. It can then put you back into a space where you can recognize that you are more empowered than you thought.

What kind of remembering does this? Remembering that you have a choice. (See what I did there?)

I am joking around a bit, because things can feel easier when they are lighter. It's also true that there is often more than one way to get to a result. If you ultimately want to build your resilience, but you feel annoyed by the idea of constantly having to learn lessons, then you can simplify it to remembering you have a choice. And choice is about empowerment, not power. Furthermore, some days you may choose not to build your resilience, simply because that's the mood you're in for whatever reason. And that's your choice.

Just as it's your choice to make a different decision and build your resilience.

This is a big step toward increasing your resilience. Unfortunately, many people forget that they have a choice in most situations, or that their life is made up of a series of decisions. Remembering that single truth can help build your resilience from the inside out. Focusing on choice helps you show up differently because it comes from empowerment; and showing up differently builds your resilience because you will be able to apply the process more easily the next time.

Resilience is something that you learn through practice. That is why you can't just learn resilience from reading, taking a class, or listening to someone. It requires your engagement, a willingness to connect with yourself in new ways, and time. Remembering that you have a choice is a tool that can help you get there, and to better understand it in this way, we can juxtapose it with holding on.

Holding vs. Remembering

When we hold on to something, we are preventing it from moving through or moving on. For example, when you hold on to a previous version of a person (perhaps a memory from high school), you are not just confining them to that past version, but you are limiting yourself and keeping yourself trapped in that old version of events (while the other person is probably not). This keeps you stuck, and you can't build resilience when you're stuck. To hold on to a grudge, an event, a memory, or a specific way of being is to keep yourself stuck. This also means that you are now the victim of your own thoughts and actions, not theirs.

Holding on requires remembering, but not in the good way— not in the way we just discussed in relation to choice. Holding on to a narrative, a thought, or a belief, is akin to cementing those items in your psyche which will never allow for the mental flexibility required to grow resilience. As we know, resilience is an inside job, and holding on to something that originated outside of you directly contradicts that, even if you've internalized it. Perhaps especially then.

Conversely, remembering without holding on can be incredibly helpful in building resilience. You can let the memory of an event inform you while you let the triggers go. With the information (i.e., due diligence), you are now free to make different choices— choices that support you in building resilience.

In this way, memory becomes a tool to support your inner growth, because you are using it to gather data or evidence on what you do or don't want in your life. In general, as a tool, memory provides you with information. Nothing more and nothing less. If you attach more significance to the memories, you might be holding on and keeping yourself out of the potential for more resilience.

Why Do We Need To Focus On Resilience?

"We must be willing to let go of the life we planned so as to have the life that is waiting for us."

– Joseph Campbell

We need to focus on resilience for all of the reasons we've already discussed, but also because our soul wants us to evolve. *We* want to evolve; it's our natural state of being. Now, we are not talking about evolving just biologically as a species or a planet; it's actually more than that.

We are hard-wired for growth, so much so that it's an inherent underlying desire.

As a species, we don't do well when things are stagnant. Though we like the security and stability of routine, we also accept that change is one of the constants of the human condition, just as it is a constant of the universe. One of the easiest ways to embrace change is to do so from curiosity—a stable, but flexible, place. This is the epitome of resilience.

Focusing on resilience is what allows us to see where we are deficient, which translates in practice to: Where can I still learn? For example, if you find yourself easily upset from small inconveniences, this is a place you can focus on to grow and evolve. Similarly, if you find yourself constantly checking social media for fear of missing out on something, this is a place where you can grow and evolve. The best way to assess where you have opportunities to grow in resilience is to identify the things that are 1) external to you and outside of your control, and 2) cause you stress.

If you are feeling stress from situations that have little to do with you or your internal life, you can see those as opportunities where you can increase your understanding and resilience. They are opportunities for you to learn new tools that can help you find more inner peace in the long run. That's resilience.

Slightly different are the opportunities that are still external but actually have something to do with your internal life. Though they are still opportunities, they can be a bit harder to learn within. If you think of the opportunities mentioned in the previous paragraph as grade school-level, then these new opportunities would be more like college-level. They are still external to you (meaning you don't control them), but because they affect you internally, they require more skill, patience, and practice. They are not the grocery store check-out line scenarios, but might be more like watching a friend make choices you know will hurt them, while not being able to do anything about it.

This is why we need to focus on resilience as something to include in our overall sense of well-being. By including resilience in the conversation, even though we cannot pursue it directly, we open the door to converting previously frustrating situations into something we can use to grow... through the lens of building resilience.

Doing so helps us evolve in a more stable, kind, and compassionate way than if we were to just stumble through everything all the time, keeping things at arm's length. In short, one of the best ways to stay aligned with who we are (as well as the higher frequency emotions that feel good) is to be resilient. Resilience helps us evolve, and it does so by making our evolution easier and more rewarding along the way.

How Do We Build Resilience?

"Resilience isn't a single skill. It's a variety of skills and coping mechanisms."

– Jean Chatzky

By now, you understand that resilience is not something you can set as a goal and take direct steps to achieve. Though you can think of it as something you want to build, you will need to take action on other goals in order to get there. Simply stated, you can't make a "to do" list for building resilience in the same way that you can make a list of things to do to lose ten pounds or train for a marathon. It's simply not tangible in the same way.

The good news about this is that resilience is a side effect or byproduct of taking action on many other things. It grows as a result of your commitment to engaging in life, which means your opportunities for creating resilience are almost endless and can happen simultaneously in more than one way at a time. The one variable you don't control, however, is time. And time is definitely part of the equation.

Resilience and Time

As with all things that are worth the wait, resilience takes time. It takes time to build the habits that create the opportunities for you to make different decisions. If we go back to the idea of standing in a check-out line, you will need to do this repeatedly (probably many times) before you really start to notice a change in your resilience. It could take weeks, months, or years, and in truth, it will probably always be evolving.

If a screaming child in a shopping cart annoys you today, you might not realize that you are no longer being annoyed by the same thing, or in the same way, until it's many years later. Furthermore, it could take even longer for you to engage kindly with the screaming child, instead of finding things to occupy your time and attention. It's all a process; the key is to begin and make time your ally.

When you make time your ally in any situation, you have unlocked a superpower. In today's culture where attention is a commodity and speed is a reward, time suddenly becomes a valuable asset. Or rather, the allowance for time becomes a valuable asset. If you are not buying into the hustle and rush that is probably flowing all around you, you are removing the externalized stimulus that can easily chip away at your resilience.

Finding Strength in the Midst of Struggle

Another part of the equation is perspective. The ability to take perspective is one of the most underestimated tools in people's toolbox. When you can take perspective—*truly* take perspective—and understand someone else's situation and position, you can make different (often better) choices. This opens up a world of possibility, including the ability to find strength in the midst of struggle.

Taking perspective is akin to being able to think outside of the box. It's a quality that is often cited in situations that require innovation or resourcefulness, but it goes beyond that. The ability to think differently creates a much larger selection of choices for any situation. You are not locked into the prescribed way of being, way of acting, or way of thinking. This is not only helpful in stressful situations, but can be beneficial in everyday life as well as serve as an example to others.[2]

Let's go back to the check-out line: If you are faced with a screaming child in a shopping cart and you take a moment to shift your perspective, you can choose to react differently. By engaging with them in a playful way, not only will you be showing the people behind you that another choice is possible, you will be helping the

---

[2] Taking perspective is addressed in greater depth in the Understanding Compassion segment.

child, too. By behaving differently and modeling resilience, you give other people permission to make a different choice in the future as well. In a world where everyone is trying to fit in and feel a sense of belonging, that is a superpower, indeed.

In short, we are more likely to work on our own resilience when we see it modeled effectively in others around us.

Resilience Is Not The Same As Resistant

"My barn having burned down, I can now see the moon."

– Mizuta Masahide

Resilience is not about weakness or strength; it's more than that. Resilience is about having tools and knowing when and how to use them. It's not about resisting life around you or rejecting a narrative that's presented to you. It's about recognizing and acknowledging life and its narratives and owning that you get to choose how you are going to show up. You are going to choose how you let life affect you. For example, you may not be able to control the weather, but you get to choose whether you are going to enjoy it, stay neutral about it, or condemn it.

For some, resisting the status quo can feel like a form of resilience, but that's usually more about power than empowerment because it's still related to something external to you. To do it in a way that is 100% about resilience would almost require a PhD in understanding resilience. The majority of people don't have that degree. Instead, if you can keep the line between internal and external clear, you have a greater chance of aligning with building resilience than reacting to an external stimulus. Ultimately, building resilience takes three things:

- Thoughtful engagement with life
- Alignment with empowerment instead of power
- Discernment in understanding what is external vs. internal

If you can keep this focus in all your daily activities and make choices that are aligned with your internal world, you can steadily build resilience. There is no inherent need for hardship and struggle to create resilience, though it is true that many do develop it that way. What's more true, though, is that simply living your daily life as a human on earth creates ample opportunities for you to increase your resilience. When you realize this, the result is a more empowered presence, which can ultimately lead to more resilience.

Conclusion

"The oak fought the wind and was broken, the willow bent when it must and survived."

– Robert Jordan

When we talk about resilience, willow trees and palm trees are often used to describe what it means in a somewhat tangible way. This is because both of these trees are fixed and flexible. They can withstand incredible winds and storms, while staying rooted to the ground. In many ways, they are the perfect metaphor for resilience. They embody the simplest definition that we often come up with, especially when looking back in hindsight.

Through the hardship of storms—through the high winds and pelting rains—these trees are living. They are still alive, still standing, and still growing. It's also true, however, that they are living through all the days that aren't stormy, that aren't rough. They live through the days that are sunny and overcast, just as they live through the days that are filled with birds and bees buzzing about. Given the ratio of stormy days to non-stormy days, it's safe to say that they live a majority of their time through life's daily ins and outs, and it's during these times that they are really building their resilience.

Willows and palm trees live through life, just as we do. Their resilience allows them to stay grounded when things get tough, but also allows them to stay grounded when things "seem" easy. I say "seem" because for all we know, they could be fighting off a fungal disease deep beneath the surface that we don't see. The same is true for humans. What we see on the outside is rarely the whole story.

Like us, the trees use their resilience every day, building on it and expanding it. They grow in resilience with every calm day and every torrential day. We can do the same. In everything we do, and everything we experience, we can build resilience. In everyday situations, this can look like having the ability to pause before speaking, or choosing not to engage with someone who is acting out until they have calmed down. It can also look like making a choice not to engage in gossip or making assumptions about something or someone without asking.

In today's modern world, it's also true that how we engage online can either build or fray our resilience. Engaging with trolls, for example, can erode your resilience, because it's not about empowerment, but about a struggle for power. If that happens, you can make a choice to return to empowerment by disengaging. When you do that, you open the door to building—and restoring—your resilience.

However resilience shows up for you, the simplest truth is that every opportunity you have to make a decision has the potential to build resilience, and you get to make those choices.

UNDERSTANDING

GRIEF

"The risk of love is loss, and the price of loss is grief.
But the pain of grief is only a shadow when
compared with the pain of never risking love."

Hilary Stanton Zunin

Introduction

"But there was no need to be ashamed of tears, for tears bore witness that a man had the greatest of courage, the courage to suffer."

– Viktor E. Frankl

Grief is a topic that everyone will need to address at some point in their lives. It's a common experience that is experienced individually. It both invites us into a new way of understanding life, while simultaneously thrusting us into changes we often don't want. It is the "push-me/pull-you" of all emotions, both causing despair in the midst of loss, while also reminding us of the depth of love or the promise of hope.

When we truly understand grief for what it is, life can somehow become easier, even though it was often hardship that brought us to this point. In that way, grief is a great teacher, and just like all teachers, it brings us lessons we may feel unready and unprepared to learn… or, perhaps, unwilling to learn.

However, when we allow ourselves to pause and become open to grief, we can find a peace that we previously didn't think possible. To understand this better, we have to break it down and truly get to the heart of what grief is, what it does, how it can benefit us, and how we can move through it, while also accepting its inherent duality: Grief is both a torment and a blessing.

What Is Grief?

"The song is ended, but the melody lingers on."
– Irving Berlin

In its simplest explanation, grief is an expression of all of the unexpressed love or hope we have for someone or something we've lost. This is why it's overwhelming at times and why we can feel "overtaken by grief."

Think of it like this: You have a reservoir of love and hope inside you that you get to share over time. As you meet people with whom you want to share your love, you connect a hose to them and start to let your love flow into them, just as their love flows back to you from their reservoir (ideally). Over the course of your life, your reservoir continually flows to people or situations in this way through small or steady doses. This allows you to experience love and hope in an ongoing way for many years.

Then, when we lose someone or something, the whole system suddenly changes. Your love is still flowing and it has to go some-where, but it can't; it's no longer attached to the other person since they're not there. So it backs up and becomes an enormous pond of all the unexpressed things we didn't get to share or do. Like a garden hose that no longer has a receptacle to fill, it just keeps flowing—so, now it's collecting inside you.

This is especially true when the loss occurs out of our expected order of things, chronologically, such as losing a child or a sibling at a young age. In those cases, the grief can feel insurmountable because there was so much love stored up in the reservoir waiting to be shared, coupled with the expectation that we would have enough time to share it.

Since the grief we carry from loss is a form of unexpressed emotion, such as love, the intensity of grief is often experienced in direct proportion to that love. In other words, the *depth of grief* now matches the *depth of the lost opportunity* to express love, or other emotions. For example, the more deeply you loved someone, the more grief you may experience when they are gone since it feels like now there is nowhere for your deep love to go. Similarly, the more unexpected the loss, the more pronounced the initial pain may be as it matches the sharp intensity of the sudden loss itself.

To further the issue, when this pool of unexpressed emotions is denied, ignored, or stuffed away, it can fester as it continues to accumulate. It needs an outlet. Therefore, all grief (regardless of its cause) requires some measure of mourning.

Whether the loss is from something tangible (like death) or less-tangible (like loss of a promotion or opportunity), you need to mourn in order to find healing and peace. The mourning process is what allows you to shift into a new perspective. Mourning is the period of time that bridges reality and acceptance, ultimately allowing you to create a new reality.

To grieve without some sort of mourning is to remain in denial; this leaves the grief in an unresolved state which can prolong it. Over time, unexpressed grief can create more problems (such as a victim identity, for example) which undermines both the possibility of finding relief from the grief as well as the potential for future happiness. Though mourning can hurt and means you have to acknowledge the loss and feel the grief, it's the healthiest way to move forward.

Let's Talk About Loss

"The bird is gone, and in what meadow does it now sing?"
– Philip K. Dick

Now that we know what grief is, we need to gain a better understanding of loss. What is loss, really? More importantly, why do we need to understand loss to understand grief? Firstly, it's worth noting that you don't have to actually lose something tangible to feel loss. Loss comes in many different shapes and sizes, but all loss triggers some form or expression of grief.

Typically, when talking about grief, the immediate assumption is that there has been a death. Grief is most closely associated with that type of loss and it's where grief is discussed most often. However, loss of any kind can trigger an experience of grief, including things like loss of opportunity. Therefore, it's important to know what loss truly means. To begin with, there are three distinct types of loss:

- Physical Loss
- Emotional Loss
- Physical and Emotional Loss

Physical Loss

This is possibly the simplest form of loss and it usually involves an object of some sort. For example, a major car accident in which your car was totaled beyond repair could trigger a sense of physical loss, just like the loss of a wedding ring in the sand on a beach holiday or someone stealing your mobile phone. Though it's about an emotional attachment in some way, this kind of loss actually requires a physical object that often represents something for the person. This is true whether it's a favorite piece of jewelry or, in a worst case scenario, the loss of a home to a fire.

In these cases, the loss that is experienced is one that triggers a sadness for the memories the object contained or the potential for what is yet to be created. The loss is tangible and experienced in real time, though it may also have lingering effects for a while, even if the item is replaced. We see this often with children who have lost a favorite stuffed animal. Their tears (and tantrums) are an expression of grief over the loss of something tangible that had significance beyond its physicality.

Emotional Loss

Different to physical loss, emotional loss implies an absence of a physical object. This type of loss is more closely related to loss of opportunity or perception. For example, if you have been planning on a promotion at work and someone else is promoted instead, this is a perceived loss. The loss is experienced entirely emotionally because it's rooted in thought and expectation. In other words, the loss is related to something that was in your mind, instead of in your environment.

More often than not, emotional loss is likened to discouragement or disempowerment, such as loss of personal agency or freedom of choice and/or thought. These are both symptoms of feeling like something has gone from you or been taken from you—often something you had previously experienced in your mind, come to expect, or hoped for.

For example, not getting into your first choice of university can be an emotional loss. The hope you once experienced in your thoughts falls away upon receipt of a rejection letter, and in its place, grief shows up as a result of the perceived loss. Emotional loss, though less tangible than physical loss, can be deeply unsettling, especially at the beginning.

Physical and Emotional Loss

This is, perhaps, the most commonly understood category of loss, because we can liken it to the majority of situations in our life.

This is the type of loss that comes from death, divorce, major change, disease or illness, financial difficulties, and so much more.

This is the loss that most of us will experience at least once in our lives, if not more. It is also the type of loss that requires more patience and understanding when dealing with grief, because it's the one that can result in a grief that lasts for the remainder of our lives.

However, even though physical and emotional loss is the most common type, it can sometimes be the least accepted and understood. This means that it also has the potential to be the least respected. Why? Because it can often trigger issues with comparative loss, which is a minefield, at best.

What Is Comparative Loss?

"Your grief path is yours alone, and no one else can walk it, and no one else can understand it."

– Terri Irwin

Comparative loss is the mechanism by which we try to create a hierarchy for the experience of loss—instead of accepting that everyone's experience is valid and unique. This is a recipe for broken relationships as well as chronic disappointment, frustration, and ultimately, resentment. The bottom line is that there is no way to accurately compare loss. There is no scale to weigh loss, because it is entirely individual.

Even though we all experience it, nobody's life experiences are exactly the same as somebody else's. Therefore, nobody can truly know what someone else is experiencing—whether it's the loss of a loved one through death or the loss of a loved one through divorce, for example. To try to compare and equate loss is to set yourself up for more hurt and damaged relationships.

Placing this type of value system on loss is to not understand it at its core: Loss is both unique and universal. Everyone experiences loss *and* everyone that experiences loss does so differently. To suggest that there is a "better" or "worse" experience of loss is to disrespect and dismiss the experience of the person who is grieving. In short, it's best not to compare loss as it rarely leads to anything positive, including healing.

The warning here is to refrain from placing a judgment on others' loss by comparing and equating it to your own or someone else's. Instead, the focus should be on understanding that loss is difficult and deeply personal and everyone needs time to mourn in their own way.

While it is kind and compassionate to understand that loss is universal, the caution comes in when saying something like, "We've both experienced loss: You've lost your family member, and I've lost my marriage or my job." Though it is true that both are examples of loss, the comparison creates a problem because it attempts to place a value on loss. If you would like to show understanding, it would be kinder to say something like, "I'm so sorry for your loss. I know how much loss can hurt. Is there anything I can do to help?"

Part of that example is about recognizing that relating to another person's loss doesn't mean you have to bring your own story into the conversation. Instead, you are saying that you know the *feeling* of loss and can relate on some level without saying that there are inherent values based on types of loss. As an example, when I lost my dog to cancer, I felt like I had lost a part of myself. For someone who doesn't like dogs, this would be unfathomable to imagine. And that's okay. Having sensitivity to another's situation is all that is required when dealing with loss and grief. Comparison (even if the intent is to try and create connection and understanding), is what's wrong. So, don't do it.

Once comparison is off the table, the one simple truth to understanding loss—and therefore understanding grief—is that everyone can relate to what it is. Though they may not know the nuanced details or emotional depth of the loss someone else is personally experiencing, everyone can understand what it feels like to go through loss. It is a human condition that very few people (if any) escape during their lifetime.

This commonality is what opens the door to understanding grief, and, more importantly, understanding how to heal.

How Long Do We Experience Grief?

"If there ever comes a day where we can't be together, keep me in your heart. I'll stay there forever."

– A.A. Milne

When does grief end? Or, does it end? These are questions most people ask when in the midst of grief, especially when relief feels out of reach. Once we understand that the essence of grief is most often tied to love, the duration of grief becomes entirely variable. For some, the grief may last until the person takes their final breath. For others, though the grief always remains, its intensity can diminish over the course of a lifetime. The grief doesn't go away; it just changes in proportion to the life you are living, the life you are adding to every day. Subsequently, there is no one answer for how long grief can last, though some have suggested that there are formulas for it.

What's important to remember is that the measure of grief will always reside in understanding its relationship to love. This can get more complicated when love is clouded by other emotions; the grief might be more drawn out or cut short.

Therefore, the best answer to the question "How long do we experience grief?" is actually: For as long as you need—or, perhaps, for as long as you want. In both instances, it takes as long as it takes, and there is no singular timeframe for grieving. There may be prescribed periods of mourning, depending on religion and culture, but grief is not the same as mourning, and how long grief lasts will always be unique to the individual undergoing it.

Understanding Mourning

Throughout history, different religious and cultural beliefs have mandated different practices for mourning. How you choose to mourn will be up to you and your specific situation. The variety of options can range significantly based on country, religion, and culture, to name a few. From ceremonies and offerings, to the specific clothing worn or number of days required to appropriately mourn the loss of someone, mourning is a very personal endeavor.

What's common among all these traditions is that mourning is inextricably linked to loss, death, and grief. What's important is to know that judging another's mourning, or imposing your type of mourning on others, is wrong.

Mourning in Relation to Death

In Western cultures, death is often not included in the discussion of life. It somehow seems counter-intuitive to talk about death when focusing on life, but nothing could be further from the truth. Death is *part* of the life cycle. Nobody escapes it, and it's completely natural. To try and tuck it away in a corner out of sight is to deny its existence.

Unfortunately, the taboo nature of discussing death contributes to the difficulty we have around truly understanding grief. Furthermore, alongside the desire to keep death out of the conversation, mourning is sometimes also sidelined. It can also seem like there is shame and judgment around mourning, specifically when discussing the why, when, where, and how long we do it. This is what happens when someone makes a passing comment like, "She's *still* not over it," or "But, it's already been a year." They think there is a prescribed way to grieve or mourn and they project it onto another by shaming them. The reverse example is also true, like when someone says, "Wow, he moved on *fast*." This is also a projection and also shame.

Of course, by not discussing grief openly (and kindly), and by keeping mourning and death at arms' length, we can unnaturally prolong the experience of grief for ourselves and others. Though there is no prescribed amount of time to grieve, there is one certainty: Judging or shaming someone, along with attempting to ignore grief or stuff it down, will most certainly extend its duration.

Mourning in Relation to Loss

Since mourning is a part of the process of healing grief, mourning also has to occur when there has been loss that isn't from death. In these cases, there may not be a prescribed religious or cultural behavior to help guide the individual undergoing loss, yet, they will still need to mourn. Examples of this kind of loss can include:

- Losing something tangible (loss of a home to a fire)
- Losing a relationship (family member, friend, romantic partner)
- Losing an opportunity (promotion, job/college acceptance)
- Losing something previously relied on (trust, belief in, or dependence on someone)

All of these losses require acknowledgment of the loss so that you can appropriately mourn. Mourning these changes in some way can help you accept them and move forward.

Grieving as a Ratio and a Rhythm

"It's possible to go on, no matter how impossible it seems, and that in time, the grief... lessens. It may not go away completely, but after a while, it's not so overwhelming."

– Nicholas Spark

There's one aspect about the duration of grief that seems to be consistent across all types and causes: Time. As long as you allow yourself to experience it, the grief will inevitably shrink in comparison to the rest of your life, if given the time.

The Ratio of Grief

Time, in this instance, is the variable that makes the grief more tolerable. It's not that the grief is actually less, but the ratio of grief to the rest of your life changes over time. As your life continues and your love for other things grows, the grief feels smaller and less consuming. Grief, therefore, is a ratio, not a fixed percentage, and the variable that changes the ratio is time.

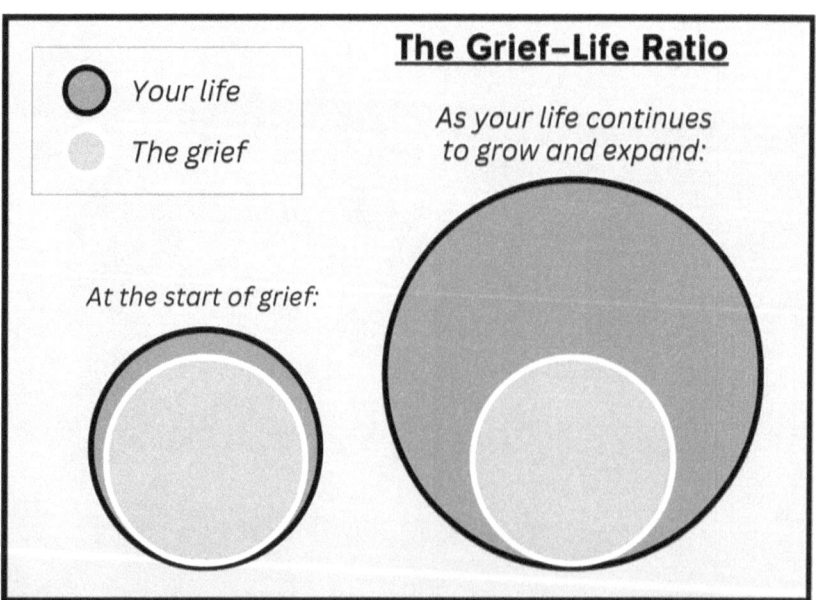

Rhythm of Grief

There's another aspect of grief that is inherent in the process regardless of the type or cause of grief: Cycles. As grief ebbs and flows in your life, it moves into a pattern—or rhythm—that you learn to live with over time as you find your footing and become better able to move with it.

For most, the grief may initially seem to come in big waves that can feel like a tsunami. You fear being drowned by them, but you somehow make it through. Then there may be a period of calm as life requires you to keep going. Over time, as the ratio changes, the waves also change. Since the process is so unique, it's as if each person's body has an inherent intelligence about how much they can handle at any given time.

Though the grief does not go away completely, it can seem to get smaller as your life continues to expand and you learn to navigate the waves and the cycles, or the rhythm, of grief.

Does grief ever go away completely? Probably not, though it can. Again, it's highly individual and therefore unique to each person experiencing it, including how much life they have invited back in, in order to move forward. This is another reason why grief can be described as a cycle.

Who Experiences Grief?

"No one ever told me that grief felt so like fear. I am not afraid, but the sensation is like being afraid."

– C.S. Lewis

If you have loved someone or something, even a little, you will experience grief at some point in your life. As we have discussed, grief is inextricably tied to love. If you have loved, or been invested in anything or anyone, you will grieve it when it goes. Of course, this statement assumes it will go at some point, which is true more often than not, because the one constant in life is change.

Since we can count on change, we can count on experiencing grief. Even though the depth and quality of the grief may vary based on the situation, you will most likely experience it—even if it's just for a moment instead of a lifetime.

Grief is a universal emotion that is experienced very individually. The simple reason for this is that we, as humans, are hardwired to need connection and expression. We have a necessity to be part of something (to belong), just as we have a need to express ourselves. To avoid this basic instinct is folly and often results in regret at the end of life. And if you think avoidance means you get to take a pass on grief, guess what? Regret is a form of grief.

Therefore, the short answer to the question "Who experiences grief?" is: Everyone. Everyone experiences grief at some point in their life, even if they don't call it that.

Other Forms of Grief

Since we know that anyone can experience grief, it stands to reason that there are other forms of grief beyond the more commonly associated expressions and experiences. These other forms of grief may not be commonly considered grief, but when we scratch beneath the surface and see that they involve loss of some kind, they usually are. This includes:

Regret, Anger, Discouragement or Disempowerment, and Frustration, to name a few.

Regret is a form of grief, because regret is usually associated with some sense of perceived loss, such as loss of opportunity or loss of self esteem. In these examples, loss of opportunity looks like wishing you had said something more to someone who is now gone, whereas loss of self esteem would be more like wishing you had said something different in a previous situation. Regret, therefore, involves an aspect of reflection coupled with a desire for something to be different in a situation outside of your control, which is why it's a type of loss.

Furthermore, until you identify the loss behind the regret and accept that you are grieving in some way, you will find it hard to move on from the feeling. Again, if there is loss, there is grief. And if there is grief, there needs to be mourning. Therefore, regret also requires some form of mourning.

Typically, when we see it in others, we meet grief with sympathy. Yet, where regret is concerned, we often treat it with disdain or dismiss it. This is also true when we are the one experiencing regret. But instead of sympathy, we should really treat regret (and grief) with empathy, because empathy is about both allowing and understanding. When it comes to another person, it's about not trying to change their thoughts or feelings and instead focusing on doing our best to relate to what they're saying while giving them space to express.

Though we may want to change things for others to try and help ease their suffering, that's not usually helpful to the person who is suffering. Instead, we can choose to sit with them through the event and validate their feelings. This is one of the most helpful things we can offer someone who is grieving, especially from regret. When it comes to us, we can use empathy to give

ourselves time and space to express while simultaneously validating what it is that we are feeling,
instead of trying to dismiss it or push it away out
of fear or guilt.

Just like all emotions tied to grief, regret needs to be
expressed and processed in order to move on. In other
words, when grief is involved, we need to allow ourselves and others the time and space required to mourn
whatever it is we have lost, or feel we have lost.

Anger can be a form of grief when it is expressed at
a time of fear. For example, when anger is about the
fear of losing something, it is a form of grief. This is
what happens when a parent yells at a child for running
away from them in a parking lot; the anger is a product
of the projected fear that comes from potentially losing
the child. The fear of loss in this case is a type of anticipatory grief expressed through anger to try and prevent
it from happening again.

Disempowerment and discouragement are forms
of grief because they are often about the loss of an
expected outcome. When there is an expectation
with an attachment to the outcome and it doesn't
come to pass, the result is often discouragement and
disempowerment, both of which require a period of
grieving to resolve.

Another form of disempowerment is marginalization,
or being dismissed. When a person's voice (perspective, contribution, and experience) is sidelined, the
resulting emotion is often one of grief expressed
through sadness, frustration, and sometimes negative
self-talk and hopelessness. These are all ways for
the unidentified grief to manifest. Instead, it would be
better to acknowledge the sense of loss, mourn it, and
then refocus. Without these steps, the manifested
emotions can turn into resentment, which can be
harder to address.

Frustration is also a form of grief on its own. This is because it usually involves some measure of unexpressed emotion. When we cannot express ourselves fully—or are not being allowed to—the result is often a feeling of not being valid, not mattering. When we are frustrated in this way, we experience a period of loss: The loss of sense of self. In order to move through this, we need to acknowledge the loss so that we can regroup and move forward with a different plan, approach, or perspective—one that allows our voices or ideas to be expressed.

Most expressions of grief are tied to loss that has already happened. This commonality makes them a universal experience and more relatable. Therefore, when thinking about who experiences grief, the answer is that we all do, or will. We all experience grief in different ways throughout our life, especially when we understand that grief is tied to loss—and loss is more pervasive than we may think. When we widen our definition of loss to go beyond death and life changes, we can see that it impacts more of our life than we may at first realize.

When we are feeling hopeless or discouraged, for example, if we pry, we can often find loss behind the proverbial curtain. Though everyone experiences grief, not everybody names it as grief. Too often, when it comes to grief, we focus on the symptom and not the cause.

The good news is that this means that we all understand loss on some level and know how to deal with it. Loss is not the same across experiences, but the tools we can use to deal with it are. By shifting our perspective to be broader, we create more capacity for resilience in the face of grief. This is true for all types of grief, including a specific one that only some of us may experience.

There is a different type of grief that affects a smaller group of people. It's a type of grief that is not necessarily tied to a tangible or identifiable loss, but it is often still tied to love. It's typically about something that hasn't happened yet, but that is believed (or feared) to be imminent. It's called Anticipatory Grief

What Is Anticipatory Grief?

"Absence is a house so vast that inside you will pass through its walls and hang pictures on the air."

– Pablo Neruda

Briefly stated, anticipatory grief is the experience of mourning before the occurrence of a tangible or identifiable loss. When we know loss is going to happen, but we don't know when, we move into a space of anticipatory grief. This is most commonly experienced with chronic and terminal illness, both on the part of the patient as well as on those who will be left behind, such as family, friends, and caretakers.

Anticipatory grief is sometimes harder to navigate because it is compounded by other emotions, such as guilt, fear, confusion, sadness, and aggravation or exhaustion, to name a few. However, the biggest of these emotions is often guilt.

A pervasive sense of guilt can often accompany anticipatory grief, predominantly because we don't understand that we are grieving, nor do we understand why or accept it as possible. The person is still with us, so it seems illogical to be experiencing grief. That thought then carries over to feelings of guilt, such as: "Why am I making this about me? I'm not the one who is ill."

But we *are* grieving. In fact, in anticipatory grief, the truth is that there are usually two layers of grief occurring at the same time:

1. Grief from the actual loss of "normal" we once shared and enjoyed with the person

2. Grief for the anticipated loss of their presence in the future

Even though someone is still alive, they may not still be alive in the same way that they once were if they are experiencing decline. This means that we are grieving the loss of ability to spend time with them in the way we always had. We've lost our sense of "normal" and are actively grieving. Additionally, as it becomes clear that there is an end on the horizon, we begin to anticipate the tangible loss of the person. Thus, we start anticipatory grieving, even if we don't name it that.

Change like this invites grief into your life in ways nothing else can. Even though we may know that our elders will one day be gone, there is no way for us to preplan our grief. Even the most mentally healthy among us will experience grief in ways we never could have anticipated once the event happens. This is why you can't plan for grief, including anticipatory grief.

The best way to deal with anticipatory grief is to identify the two aspects that are influencing your emotions, and then allow yourself to process them while giving yourself permission to mourn.

- It is okay to mourn the loss of somebody before they're physically gone from your life, in fact, it's important that you do. When you identify that you are mourning the loss of how things used to be, you are better able to show up with empathy and kindness for yourself and them.

- It is also okay to mourn the projections you are experiencing when you think about a future without them in your life. By acknowledging that you will be affected by this loss, it can help you focus on the present and enjoy their company now.

Regardless of whether it's traditional grief or anticipatory grief, the underlying truth remains the same: Grief is highly individual and personal. Since we will all experience grief at some point in our lives (often multiple times), we must accept this truth in order to be flexible and move with it. This means that everyone experiences grief and there is no one way to express or deal with it. Acceptance of this truth gives us all the freedom we need to mourn and grieve, which is what ultimately helps us heal.

How Do We Express Grief?

"To weep is to make less the depth of grief."
– William Shakespeare

Depending on your culture, beliefs, and situation, your expression of grief may vary. This is to say that different people, communities, and societies express grief in different ways, and none are better or worse than the other. As such, we can instead look at where we express grief in our bodies, which can transcend any society, practice, or culture.

Grief is most commonly expressed through tears. When we are overcome by grief and sadness, we cry. It is suggested that when we release tears, our body receives this as a signal to also release feel-good chemicals, like endorphins and oxytocin.

These feel-good chemicals help to regulate our system as we move through the phases of grief. They also serve to help us physically, because when we are in grief, we can actually hurt or feel pain in our bodies. This is why grief is often related to statements like, "broken-hearted" or "my heart hurts." Underneath everything else, we are sensory beings.

One of the ways we are able to make sense of the world is through our interactions with it on a physical level, which includes our five senses.

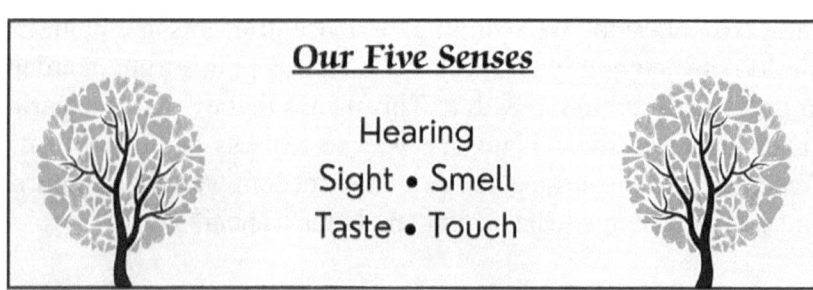

Our Five Senses

Hearing
Sight • Smell
Taste • Touch

As sensory beings, it stands to reason that we need to process our emotions physically, as well as mentally and emotionally. This means that regardless of the type of grief we are experiencing (physical, emotional, or both), we need to use our physical being to help us process the loss because that's how we're made.

The pain we feel is a signal to our brains that it's time to do something physical to help process the overwhelming emotion. Sometimes, we do this through physical activity, such as running, cleaning, or sobbing. But we also do it through less-healthy endeavors such as over-eating or starving ourselves, sex, and engaging in numbing activities, like gaming or binge-watching media. When we don't process our grief (or other emotions), it can show up dysfunctionally, including lashing out at others.

The bottom line is that if we don't actively work to identify, acknowledge, and process our grief, it will still find a way to be expressed. When that happens, it often comes out of us sideways. This is what can ultimately damage relationships the most, leading to more potential loss... and more grief.

Expressing grief in healthy ways—through physical, mental, and emotional means—is the best way to give yourself the help you need to heal. How you choose to grieve is up to you; nobody can do it for you, nor choose for you. The most important thing you can do is allow yourself to grieve. Give yourself permission to take the time and space you need to listen to your heart, feel the grief, and express it. Feeling grief in your body is normal and it requires a tangible approach to healing. A healthy intervention can include things like: movement, counseling, journaling, and practicing self-care.

Unfortunately, sometimes there is a stigma around expressing grief, such as when someone thinks your grief "should be over because enough time has passed." Even if these statements are made with the best of intentions (wanting you to feel better), as a society, we would do well to normalize grief as part of life. When we understand that it already is, we become more accepting of others' journeys through grief, which may, in turn, help them move through the most intense aspects of grieving with more grace.

The first step of any grief journey is to understand that you are a sensory being, which means that you have the capacity to feel grief in multiple ways and probably will. By accepting this, you become better able to manage and move through grief.

The second step is to find outlets for your grief—whether they are group-related or individual outlets does not matter. What you want to focus on is finding things that support you in your grieving process, whatever that looks like for you.

Why Do We Grieve?

"Happiness is beneficial for the body, but it is grief that develops the powers of the mind."

– Marcel Proust

We grieve because our minds and bodies need to express the emotion behind loss. That is the simplest answer. The more complex answer takes in the bigger picture, including an aspect of needing to make sense of something that we possibly don't want—or aren't ready and willing—to accept. Grief makes living with loss possible.

How does it do this? By creating a change within us: The grieving period gives us time to shift from denial to acceptance.

Grief is a common experience. We all understand it, even if we understand it differently in its nuances and expressions. Sometimes, we can know when someone else is experiencing grief just by looking at them. This is because we know grief, as individuals and as humans. We also know grief enough to be able to see it in other species.

For example, wildlife researchers have identified elephant grieving behaviors such as: holding vigil, touching, making noise, and showing reverence. When we watch elephants in videos, we can relate to their grief at the loss of a member of the pack. Or when we see dogs lie on their owner's grave, we know this is a sign of grieving. We may be anthropomorphizing the animal, but we do so because we know grief when we see it, even across species.

So, why do we grieve? What purpose does grief serve? By now, you know that grief serves to bring us to acceptance by bridging the gap from one reality to a new reality. It also helps us process emotions to help ourselves heal, especially when it prompts our brain to release feel-good chemicals. This is survival at its best. Our brain wants to keep us alive and may see an overflow of emotions as a potential threat to our survival, so it fixes it by releasing chemicals to help. There is, however, more to discuss when it comes to grief, including the two extremes at either end of the spectrum of grief:

- Grief and depression
- Grief avoidance or not feeling the need to grieve

Grief and Depression

Everyone handles loss differently. We know this to be true. For some, the experience of grief can lead to something more seemingly permanent: depression. It's important to note that a clinical diagnosis of depression is different from a person who is cycling through grief in ways that keep them stuck in the cycle. There are specific clinical measurements that a trained mental health professional must use to properly diagnose depression, especially Major Depressive Disorder (MDD). In such cases, working with a professional is important.

Where grief is concerned, it is helpful to know that grief does not automatically lead to depression, though they can share symptoms or look similar. To understand this better, we can differentiate the two by noting that grief can typically be tied to loss of some kind, whereas depression does not need a loss correlation.

So, what is going on when a person appears to be "grieving" endlessly and in ways that mimic a depressive episode? Sadly, I have at times heard this referred to as self-indulgent, which it is not. It would be more accurate to say that it's the body's way of trying to process something it just can't understand or accept. Let's return to an earlier statement: The grieving process (which includes mourning) allows us to shift from denial to acceptance.

If the loss is never fully accepted, then it may not be just grief that they are experiencing, but chronic sadness and even fear. This state of being can cycle endlessly and lead the person to a form of persistent situational depression. For this, they will need more help from professionals, possibly including medication. Medicinal treatment for mental health is often stigmatized, but it shouldn't be. The body is made up of chemicals, and if some of those chemicals are over-firing or not firing at all, the body may need medicinal support to rebalance. When a person is chronically cycling through loss in ways that share symptoms with depression (or, in fact, if the loss triggers depression), then medicinal support is not only warranted, but it could be life-changing. Additionally, if a person seems to be stuck in the cycle of loss and sadness from grief, it may be time to intervene in other ways to give them the support they need to come to a place of acceptance.

Sometimes, the reluctance to come to acceptance has its roots in fear or guilt—feeling guilty for "moving on" from the loss. This can be especially true if the person is experiencing "survivor's guilt" or if the loss was sudden and wholly unexpected, such as with suicide. When this occurs, it can be helpful to explain that acceptance does not mean that you no longer feel the loss; it means that you are able to put the loss into context in a way that allows you to move through the grief to arrive at the new reality. Even though grief may never fully leave, the quality of the grief can change over time. This can be the shift an individual needs to break the cycle of chronic sadness as a result of loss.

Conversely, at the other end of the spectrum, there are some individuals who may not feel the need to grieve, even though they have experienced loss. Though this may seem uncommon, it may not be as rare as you think. In these cases, it is just as important to support the individual in their process, without judging or imposing your own beliefs and ideas on them. Why does this matter? Because just as we need to normalize expressions of grief, we also need to accept and normalize that not everybody feels the need to grieve, whether it's right now, or ever.

What if I Don't Feel the Need to Grieve?

As we know, there is no singular-prescribed period or process for grief. This also means that there is nothing "wrong" with someone who does not feel the need to grieve. Just as there is nothing wrong with someone who feels the need to grieve differently than you. Unfortunately, we often project our own expectations and understanding of grief on others, which can lead to experiences of shame or guilt for not grieving or for grieving too much or in the wrong ways.

If someone does not feel the need to grieve a loss, the best thing to do is to support them in this decision. There may be many reasons why this is their experience or choice, such as:

- They are in denial, and need to remain there for the foreseeable future to protect their mental health. This could mean that they will grieve eventually, once they have more mental and emotional space, or it could mean that they never grieve this particular loss.

- The nature of their relationship to what was lost is not what it appeared to be. This is particularly apt when we hear someone speaking ill of a person who has died. If a death brings a sense of freedom to the person who is left behind, then it's likely that others have made assumptions about their relationship if they are surprised by this reaction.

- They process grief differently. This is more common across cultural and religious divides, but not solely. There are people who have done so much self-work that they process grief very quickly and internally, which can look like they are not grieving to others. They may be grieving, or they may not be grieving. Either way, it's entirely personal.

Of course, there are many more reasons why someone may not feel the need to grieve. What matters is that we are accepting of the individual's choice and we provide support and understanding along the way. Someone who does not feel the need to grieve now may suddenly be blind-sided by grief at a distant point in the future. They will need support and understanding. Similarly, someone who is stuck in a cycle of loss and sadness also needs support and understanding.

When we understand that we grieve to make sense of something that is outside of our control—to bring us from denial to acceptance—we are better able to not only process our own grief but also be supportive of others who are grieving.

How Can I Heal From Grief?

"You will survive, and you will find purpose in the chaos. Moving on doesn't mean letting go."

– Mary VanHaute

Healing from grief is a process. There is no magic wand, no specific timeline, and no pill or prescription you can take to "fix" your grief. The good news is that there is one certainty about grief: If you allow yourself to move through it, it changes. That is to say that the quality and quantity of the grief you experience changes.

Over time, though you may still be able to tap into the original sensation of grief and be able to identify and feel loss on a regular basis, it still changes. It becomes less intense when you allow yourself to process it and flow with it.

Conversely, when you try to tamp it down, stuff it away, or make it rigid by trying to fit it into a specific box or framework, it can become more consuming and more fixed in your being. This is often what happens when you see someone constantly cycling through the loss.

Healing from grief, like all emotions, needs you to be willing. It requires your active participation as well as your flexibility. In order to heal, you need to both address it and not fixate on it. In other words, you need to identify it, work with it when it arises, and when it fades from view for a little while, you need to allow it to do so without guilt. By engaging in this dance with grief, you begin to heal. Your acceptance of grief as a part of life, allowing it to ebb and flow, is what ultimately allows you to heal over time.

Unfortunately, we can feel guilty when we suddenly realize we are laughing, even though we have lost someone. Often, the remedy for the guilt is to put our attention back on the loss. Sometimes this is a good idea (if it's brief and temporary), and sometimes it's not (if it's consuming). By allowing ourselves to flow with the emotions and thoughts that arise, we give ourselves permission to continue to participate in life, even when we are in the midst of grief. As a result, we become more resilient, more empathic, and more understanding of ourselves and others.

This, ultimately, is what leads to healing from grief... and almost anything, actually. The goal is not to live without grief; the goal is to understand that it's okay to live with grief and to keep living—to experience life, even in the face of loss, and enjoy it.

More Notes On Grief

"We all want to do something to mitigate the pain of loss or to turn grief into something positive, to find a silver lining in the clouds. But I believe there is real value in just standing there, being still, being sad."

– John Green

Grief is universal, and when it's universally understood, we may feel a need to help. But we also need to be cautious about taking on someone else's grief. As kind and thoughtful humans, when we see someone in pain, we can have a tendency to want to "fix" it. Though this may feel like a thoughtful gesture, unless you are a healthcare professional in an emergency room, it's not actually helpful in the long run.

Taking on someone else's grief looks like doing things for them so that they don't feel the emotional waves. In other words, you try to redirect the tsunami, often toward yourself, in order to prevent them from feeling pain. However, when you do this, you are denying them the opportunity to move into acceptance. You are also limiting their potential. You are taking away their chance to improve their resilience and become happier in their life. It may seem counterintuitive, but it's true.

Allowing someone to experience their grief is not only necessary, it's imperative for their acceptance of the new reality as well as their growth, mentally, emotionally, and even physically. By experiencing grief and learning how to navigate through it, they are building tools that they can use in the future to create a healthier and better life.

So, what can you do when you see someone hurting from grief?

Instead of doing things *for* them, you do things *with* them. You can sit with them. You can draw on your own experience of grief and show compassion and understanding. If needed, you can provide resources as suggestions, not tasks to complete. In short, you can do things to be with them—which may be more valuable than anything else you can provide.

Resources For Grief

"No matter how long it's been, there are times when it suddenly becomes harder to breathe."

– Anonymous

Though there are many resources available to people experiencing grief, there are two that stand above the rest: Process/Grief Groups and Journaling. This is because one helps you to connect with others so that you feel less alone in your journey and the other helps you to connect with yourself so that you can begin to make sense of your feelings. Both can be incredibly helpful to anyone experiencing grief.

- **Process/Grief Groups**–Attending a grief or process group helps in multiple ways, but perhaps the most important is that it can help to normalize the grief experience, making us feel less alone. The desire for connection is ingrained in our human nature. As such, we crave a sense of belonging.

  When we undergo something that changes our world and our life in significant ways, it is incredibly helpful to feel like we are still part of something. The grief group provides a safe space to share feelings, fears, and thoughts regarding a significant life event. It also gives language to the experience that we might not otherwise have.

  Being able to speak to the grief using words that help it all make sense is incredibly important, especially when it comes to being able to express our needs and expectations to others in our life.

- **Journaling**–Whether it's free-form or prompted, journaling is something that can really help us understand our thoughts and feelings. It allows us to process what's going on in our heads and our bodies in a safe way, in our own time, and at a pace that we need. It's also incredibly flexible.

You can journal anywhere at any time. There is no limit to how, when, or where you can write. There are also multiple ways you can journal, from using actual pen and paper, to creating a digital journal on your devices. The only caution would be ensuring that both a paper and a digital journal are protected so that they remain confidential.

Once you have done this, journaling is a highly effective way to navigate the ups and downs of grief, helping you to make sense of the situation and move from denial to acceptance.

Regardless of whether you are moving through grief yourself or helping someone else, the most important thing to remember is that it is a highly individual experience. Keeping this simple truth in mind will allow you to have more grace in both situations, which is good for everyone.

Conclusion

"When you are sorrowful look again in your heart, and you shall see that in truth you are weeping for that which has been your delight."

– Khalil Gibran

Understanding grief is about understanding that all humans are different while also being similar. Grief is one of the most universally-experienced emotions, and yet, it can be expressed in almost as many ways as there are people on the planet. Where there is overlap, we find aspects of community, religion, society, culture, and tradition. But the actual internalized experience will always be unique to the person going through it.

More often than not, to be in grief is to have loved. To experience grief is to know loss. To move through grief is to grow. Through grief, we build resilience, compassion, and understanding. Through grief, we honor the love we are capable of feeling for someone or something. Through grief, we gain a deeper sense of what we value and hold dear.

If you don't know if you're experiencing grief, but you feel out of sorts from a situation, ask yourself if you are experiencing loss. Since loss can take many forms, including things we may not normally think of, being able to identify it is key to healing. Once you've identified something as loss, you can now allow yourself the time and process you need to mourn so that you can heal.

It is nearly impossible to live a life in which you don't grieve. In this way, grief, above all else, is both the price we pay for being human, as well as one of life's greatest gifts. Because a life without grief potentially also means a life without love, without investment, without passion, joy, and hope. Grief reminds us that we are alive, that we are all connected, and that we have loved and can love. It helps us remember that we can invest in both the people and experiences that bring us joy, even though we know we can also lose them.

Grief, therefore, is the ultimate teacher of what it means to be human. When we can move through grief and get to a place where we understand it and learn how to live with it, we suddenly realize what it means to truly live… and our life is all the better for it.

UNDERSTANDING

COMPASSION

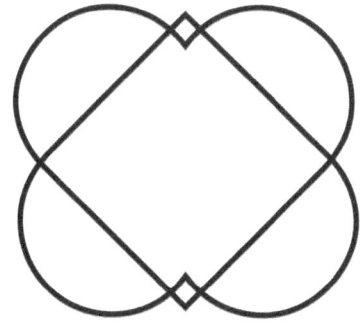

"Love and Compassion are necessities, not luxuries.
Without them humanity cannot survive."

Dalai Lama

Introduction

*"The purpose of human life is to serve, and to show com-
passion and the will to help others."*

– Albert Schweitzer

Compassion is a topic that can feel incredibly subjective, though
the ample research implies some measure of objectivity. In the
early 2000s, Dr. Kristin Neff pioneered the first empirical studies
of self-compassion after becoming interested in the practice
alongside Buddhism. Considered the foremost authority on the
subject, Dr. Neff's work subsequently prompted thousands of
studies by other researchers. This volume of research suggests
that self-compassion is both measurable (quantifiable) and tangible (qualitative). But self-compassion is not the compassion
we are discussing here; it is a *type* of compassion, or a directed
expression of compassion. So, what is *compassion?*

The Oxford English Dictionary cites the first use of the word
"compassion" in 1340, as: *"Suffering together with another,
participation in suffering; fellow-feeling, sympathy."* Though
this definition is currently considered obsolete, the notion of
"fellow-feeling" is still an integral piece of the puzzle.

Colloquially, the word "compassion" has evolved to imply a
measure of separated concern, such as pity. (e.g. "Have pity on
them; show some compassion.") While this may seem true, it's
not the whole story. Nor is pity the same as compassion. In order
to truly understand compassion, we must also understand its
various components, most of which involve some measure of
fellow-feeling. These include: sympathy, empathy, care, and
perspective.

For compassion is not just one thing; it's an interplay between
various components that engenders both thought and feeling in a
way that is greater than the sum of its parts.

What Is Compassion?

"Compassion is the ultimate expression of your highest self."
– Russell Simmons

When we talk about compassion, we need to first understand both the players and the components. Unlike with self-compassion, when we are discussing compassion, we need to have more than one person or entity involved. Its very nature is dependent on there being at least two players, hence the "fellow-feeling" aspect of compassion still remaining true to this day.

The Players

In any given situation where there is compassion, there are always at least two groups or entities involved. For ease of understanding, we will call these the Giver and the Receiver. Both the Giver and the Receiver can be individuals or groups, in any combination.

The Giver is the person or group that feels concern and/or care for the Receiver. This can be as a result of a situation or circumstance, or a long-standing hierarchy (noblesse oblige, for example). It requires the Giver to express an emotion toward the Receiver in a way that implies either sympathy or empathy (more on the difference between the two in a moment). That emotion can then prompt action, or not. Contrary to common belief, compassion does not always lead to a change in behavior, though it often can.

The Receiver is, therefore, the recipient of the Giver's attention and focus. Sometimes, they benefit from the Giver's awareness and compassion, sometimes they don't. The benefit can be lasting or temporary, based on the situation, and often involves some measure of gratitude on the part of the Receiver, though it is not usually a requirement for receipt.

For example, an unhoused person sitting on a city sidewalk with an open cup may receive money from passers-by as an expression of compassion. While they may respond with a gentle nod or "thank you," it is not a requirement for the gift of charity. Similarly, an entire community that receives a new water well and pump from a charitable organization may feel gratitude toward the group, but may not necessarily express that gratitude directly to the donors to the organization. Nor is the expression of gratitude a requirement of the donation.

Another good example of this is when the Receiver is a living being, but not a human being. In this scenario, the Giver focuses their attention on charitable organizations that support the welfare of animals or environments. Though they may be thanked for their gift of time or resources, the ultimate recipients (i.e. the animals) may not even be aware of the Givers' existence.

Most importantly, an expression of compassion is made freely by a Giver, without any expectation of return from the Receiver. In all of these scenarios, there are always at least two participants when it comes to compassion. So, now that we know about the players, what are the components involved?

The Components

As previously mentioned, there are primary components that work together to create what we call compassion. Though there may be more, the four most important ones are: Perspective, Sympathy, Empathy, and Care.

These four components are not mutually exclusive and can occur in any combination often with other emotions or experience, which is partially what makes compassion so subjective. It's also why if you ask people to define "compassion," you usually get multiple answers with various qualifiers. If you break it down, however, those answers probably all revolve around some aspect of these four primary components.

Of the four, it's fair to say that there is one that stands above the rest as a requirement for compassion. You may be inclined to think it's "care," but the truth is, it's perspective. Or, more accurately, it's the ability—*and desire*—to take perspective. This is true even if the Giver isn't consciously aware that they are doing so.

As such, in order to truly understand compassion, we need to start with understanding what it means to "take perspective."

Taking Perspective

"In separateness lies the world's greatest misery; in com-passion lies the world's true strength."

– Buddha

The ability to take perspective is a superpower. Full stop. It is one of the most important skills you can acquire in life and possibly the most important tool in your emotional toolbox. If there were a manual for how to succeed at life and be a good human being, it would be listed in the first three steps; it's that important.

Unfortunately, it's not often talked about in this way, and it can sometimes even be disparaged (most often when it is misunderstood and thought of as a weakness). But, if you study the behavior of individuals with high emotional intelligence, it's likely that they all know how to take perspective and probably practice it quite regularly and even subconsciously.

Why is it so important, though? What does it do for us, individually, and as a whole?

In order to understand why this is so important, we need to first accept that it is part of human nature to belong to a group. We require connection and a sense of belonging in order to survive, live, and thrive. It's a biological drive that is true for the vast majority of people on the planet. This need means that we have to be a *part of* something, not *apart from* something.

If we are left out of the group, we risk dying. It's that simple. Even though we are no longer "hunter-gatherers" in our daily life, meaning we no longer need to rely on the group to eat or survive, we are still genetically hard-wired to belong.

And, what makes it easier to belong? The ability to take perspective.

It is an evolutionary skill that has allowed us to make belonging easier. Think about it like this: The last time you underwent some sort of crisis or suffering, it was probably the person who related to you the most that helped you to feel better. They related to you because they could understand your perspective, either from experience or because they have honed their ability to do so.

A Part vs. Apart

These words are often used incorrectly and interchangeably as many assume they are synonyms simply because they sound the same. The truth is they are opposites.

If you are "a part of" something, it means you are connected to it and probably invested in it in some way. For example if you are a part of a team, you want the team to win or succeed at whatever it is doing. You have an interest in seeing things work out. You are a member; you belong.

If, however, you are "apart from" something, it means you are not including yourself in it. Additionally, you are most likely making a statement to make it clear that you are not a part of it and probably not invested in it. You may even have a desire to see things not work out. In other words, it's not something you belong to.

Taking perspective results in an ability to connect, and an ability to connect results in a stronger, healthier group overall. At its core, taking perspective is an evolved survival method. This means that the reverse is also true. Someone who can't take perspective may be unable to connect, which can result in their being ostracized or left on the fringes of the group. Their inability to relate has ramifications for them personally and for the larger group, as a whole.

Now, let's take a look at the impact this skill can have on ourselves as well as others, beyond the obvious benefit of connection.

Perspective and Emotional Evolution

One of the simplest truths about humans is that we are designed to evolve, just like the rest of nature. We are not excused from the biological patterns inherent in being a living being, even though some humans may behave as if they are. Biological evolution, at its core, is a very slow process, often taking many generations to show even the smallest shift.

However, there are other forms of evolution that we rarely discuss that humans have somehow managed to hardwire to be faster. Primarily, this includes emotional and mental evolution. The result of mental evolution, which involves the brain and its innovative capacity, is most often seen in technological advances as well as a deeper understanding of concepts and ideas.

Emotional evolution is different. It's also a bit more of a minefield, because true emotional evolution involves some measure of trial and failure in order to build resilience and deepen understanding. Unfortunately, there are many practices and teachings that use "bypassing" in order to achieve the appearance of emotional evolution. When we bypass something, however, we are not learning or evolving; we are simply using a cheat sheet thinking that if we give the "correct" answer to something, we will have evolved. But emotional evolution happens in the learning and practicing, in the failing and trying, not in the (re)iteration of an answer.

So, what does this mean when it comes to perspective?

To begin with, the ability to take perspective protects the group. When the group is protected, the individual feels safe. When individuals feel safe they are better able to engage in practices that lead to emotional evolution, both together and alone. This translates to an emotionally evolving group at an exponential pace as the group becomes greater than the sum of its individual parts.

Now, imagine having multiple groups all engaging in emotional evolution in this way. The result is a stronger, more emotionally balanced and healthy society. Move forward some more, and we have stronger communities, countries, and a healthier planet overall. Why? Because when everyone is able to engage in individual emotional evolution, we create pathways for emotional evolution for the whole. Somewhere along the way, even though the initial practice may have been a solo endeavor, the focus shifts from being me-based to we-based, because people feel supported by one another. That support comes from connection and the connection has its roots in the ability to take perspective.

Taking perspective naturally invites compassion into the conversation—including when taking perspective on your own life. Sometimes, when we feel lost or are struggling, taking a step back to get out of the weeds and get a wider view is the shift we need to see things in a new way and make a different decision. As an added benefit when we do this for others, not only can we see ourselves in their shoes and relate, but we can also help them by accessing that wider view when/if they can't.

Taking perspective involves being able to put yourself into the other's situation. It requires you to set your own experiences, prejudices, and biases aside so that you can access what it might feel like to live as the other, even for the briefest moment. The interplay between the self and the other takes on new meaning when we can see everything and everyone as part of a whole. Compassion invites us to remember connection, just as connection invites us to be compassionate.

Once we are able to take perspective, a world of options opens up to us when it comes to compassion. These options include the other primary components of compassion: Sympathy, Empathy, and Care.

What Does It Mean To Care?

"We forget some of the oldest medicines we have are love and compassion, and they can be deployed by everyone."

– Vivek Murthy

Care, simply stated, means to feel concern for. Though there may be variations on this theme, to care for someone or something means you are concerned for it, and most likely for its well-being. Though it can often be equated to love, it doesn't have to be. You can care for anything (like your home, your garden, or your floors), or anyone (like family, friends, and disenfranchised groups).

Care has no limits to its application, which is why it is a key component of compassion. It also requires two players (unless it's self-care, then it's like self-compassion). However, when it comes to care, the two players do not both need to be living beings. Care can involve inanimate objects, just as it can be focused on the living. For the purpose of the discussion on compassion, we will limit ourselves to the care expressed between living beings.

For the most part, we mostly see care as part of relationships. These can be platonic, familial, romantic, or anything that involves at least two people or groups. In fact, as a general rule, relationships often involve an unspoken agreement of care.

Of course, there are professional relationships that also involve care, but in those instances, the arrangement is not left unsaid; it's usually written out and negotiated. For example, a homecare nurse has a specific contract to provide services in exchange for a fee. Everything will be discussed and negotiated as part of a care agreement.

That being said, regardless of the type of relationship (professional or relational), most care-based situations create, or result in, some measure of compassion. There is a specific type of care, however, that usually requires compassion from the onset, not as a result: Being a caregiver. Because it's becoming more common as populations live longer, let's take a moment to explore this subcategory of care.

~~~~~

As many people around the world are aging, we are seeing a marked increase in the need for at-home caregivers. These can be professionals or volunteers who come into the home to offer support and services, but more often than not, they are family members or relatives. If the latter, the caregiving role often goes beyond the basic premise of "care and concern"—it requires deep compassion.

Caregiving, therefore, is something that sits outside the general definition of caring. In other words, just like care is a necessary component of compassion, compassion is a necessary component of care*giving*. In this way, the cause/effect relationship between the two has shifted to one that is more of a "chicken-egg" situation. Furthermore, when one wanes, it seems to directly (and often negatively) affect the other. They are inextricably intertwined, both needing the other in order to maintain a given situation. While this is the case for most family caregivers, it's especially true for Sideline Caregivers.

What is a Sideline Caregiver?

A Sideline Caregiver is a person who has all (or most) of the responsibility and none (or little) of the agency in caring for another person. Think of a player on the sidelines of any game. Their job is to "participate" in the game by watching every move as if they were on the field so that they can be ready to jump in, if needed. They cannot sit down on the bench and play on their phone, nor can they leave the sideline, just in case they are needed. They are a passive player until they're not, and they don't get to choose when that changes.

Many people in the "sandwich generation" are finding themselves becoming Sideline Caregivers while they are still in the process of raising a family. There are probably even more people who are new empty-nesters that are now finding themselves in this unexpected role. And just like an understudy in a play or musical, they have to learn their part (or multiple parts) in order to be ready to take over at a moment's notice, often without warning or consideration.

For this group, caring and compassion are part of the equation from the start. The reason that being a Sideline Caregiver might be more exhausting than being a regular caregiver is because of the imbalance between agency and responsibility, as well as the perpetual state of not knowing. Sideline Caregivers don't know when things will change, they just expect that it will at some point and the balance will shift. In essence, they are waiting for the other proverbial shoe to drop, which may (or may never) happen. And unlike understudies or replacement players, this isn't their only role, nor are they being compensated for it, further underscoring how significant care and compassion are in this scenario.

Finally, this role requires both compassion *and* self-compassion (often in the form of self-care) for the Sideline Caregiver to try and maintain some semblance of mental, emotional, and physical health.

Ultimately, care—or caring—is a key component of compassion, mainly because *not* caring is an expression of disengagement, detachment, or disinterest. Compassionate behavior is an expression of investment, of recognizing that there is something more—that everything ultimately affects everything else in some way. To have compassion is to care.

How you care is up to you, and two of the most common ways are through sympathy and empathy.

Sympathy vs. Empathy

"Empathy is seeing with the eyes of another, listening with the ears of another, and feeling with the heart of another."

– Alfred Adler

In recent years, much has been discussed around the subject of empathy, mainly due to the viral success of Dr. Brené Brown's TED Talk in 2010: *The Power of Vulnerability*. In her research, Dr. Brown gave new language to the relationship between vulnerability, courage, empathy, and shame, resulting in millions around the world having "A-ha!" moments that led them to create positive change in their lives, which is always a good thing.

Having studied with Brené in graduate school in 2012, I had a lightbulb moment in her class when she described the difference between sympathy and empathy using a *really* easy to understand example (roughly paraphrased here, as I remember it):

Sympathy is like seeing a friend stuck in a deep hole with no way out, looking down at them and saying, "I'm so sorry," while staying safe where you are. You can feel genuine concern for them, but they (or their situation) remains solidly outside of your own... by choice.

Empathy is like seeing a friend in that same hole, finding a ladder to climb down to them (while also ensuring that the ladder is there as a way out for you), sitting down beside them in their situation and simply saying, "I'm sorry... and I get it," while giving them the space and time they need to process whatever it is they're going through (i.e. not forcing them to stand up and get out of the hole or trying to fix it).

In other words, empathy involves relating. Refer back to the segment on perspective: Without the ability to take perspective (either through direct experience or honed skill), empathy is *much* harder to achieve. In Brené's scenario, a key piece is knowing that you can get back out of the hole, even if your friend doesn't want to. It's a crucial element of empathy, actually. Being able to relate does not mean being emotionally taken down. That's not relating, and that's not empathy.

That moment in class was a personal "A-ha!" for me, because I had never been able to easily explain the difference between the two until that day—even though I knew there was one, since I had experienced it when my father had his stroke a few years earlier.

In the first couple of days while my dad lay in the ICU, a lot of people came to the hospital to visit us. However, there was one person who stood out in his response to the situation. Unlike everyone else who offered their condolences and loving thoughts (which was nice), this friend of my sister's showed up, put his hands on my shoulders and said simply, "This sucks." He got it. In that single moment, I felt seen, understood, and supported. That's empathy.

When it comes to compassion, you need to understand the difference so that you can make a choice on how to act. It's not helpful to anyone if, for example, you would become emotionally undone by being empathetic.[3] In that instance, you might choose sympathy over empathy as part of your expression of compassion. If, however, you feel the need to sit with someone in their despair, knowing that you can step away and be okay, then empathy might be your preferred expression of compassion.

What's true is that compassion typically requires either empathy or sympathy, which means it requires you to show up. How you choose to show up is up to you and is based on your ability and resources, including your emotional and mental resources. To better understand this, let's describe a different, yet tangible, scenario:

> *Compassion with empathy* might look like working in
> a soup kitchen and sitting with the clients to talk with

---

[3] I wrote about the difference between "empathetic" and "empathic" on my Substack if you would like to learn more.

them as they enjoy a warm meal, while *compassion with sympathy* might look like sending supplies or resources to the soup kitchen or helping with administrative duties.

Both are examples of compassion in action, and both are helpful to the Receiver, which means one is not better than the other in that regard. Additionally, both mean you are a Giver. When it comes to compassion, what matters is that you are doing what you are capable of doing so that you can continue to be a Giver.

Compassion And Pity

"Tolerance and compassion are qualities of fearless people."
– Paulo Coelho

In order to truly understand compassion at its core, it can be helpful to juxtapose it with pity. Though they can sometimes seem like synonyms, at their closest they are actually more like two sides of a coin. In action, however, they are incredibly different and the purity of true compassion bears little resemblance to an expression of pity. Much like sympathy and empathy can sometimes seem similar in appearance but are different at their core, compassion and pity have a tendency to emulate each other, but their roots are actually opposites.

Let's start with pity.

Like compassion, pity often involves an expression of concern and care. However, it usually incorporates something else. Pity is commonly defined as "sympathetic sorrow for one suffering, distressed, or unhappy."[4] As such, it is often accompanied with an underlying plea for mercy or grace (as in "take pity on me"). Though we may think we meet requests for pity with compassion, is that really true?

If someone asks for your pity, how are you responding? What are your first thoughts? Is there an element of judgment in your assessment? Do you subconsciously take a moral inventory to gauge whether the person is deemed worthy of your care and concern? Then, are you taking pity on them? In other words, do you feel sorry for them? If so, you'd more likely be offering sympathy than empathy, which prompts another question: Are you sitting with them or are you holding them apart? Finally, how do you feel when you offer someone pity in the form of concern?

I'd suggest that it's in how we feel when we are offering our care and concern to others that we notice the real difference

---

[4] Merriam-Webster. (n.d.). Pity definition & meaning. Merriam-Webster.com. Retrieved on 23 August 2025.

between pity and compassion. Pity is often aligned with emotions and ego—with a value system of some sort. In some cases, if we are feeling pity for someone, there is a possibility that we are also feeling relief that it's not us, making it even more hierarchical. Furthermore, if we are offering assistance because we feel pity, it's possible that our egos are getting a boost because of the "good" thing we are doing.

Over the years, I have come to see pity as a very externally-aligned endeavor. Yes, it can have a positive impact on the recipient: A donation is a donation, after all, and if you're hungry you welcome almost any form of assistance. But for the giver, an expression of pity is often part of something externalized to the self, inviting in feelings of esteem or self-worth through external measurements. More so, we can often attach to a desired outcome when pity is involved. We want to see things change *because* we intervened. Then, if they don't (especially not in the way we expected or wanted), we might be less inclined to help in the future.

Pity, though it can sometimes look like compassion or feel compassionate to the recipient who is struggling and welcomes any form of assistance, is often tainted by some measure of self-interest.

Compassion—true compassion—is the opposite. At its core, it's neutral. It has its roots in purity of intention, which means there is rarely, if ever, an attachment to it. It's giving for giving's sake, or helping for helping's sake, and nothing more. It requires no emotional investment on an ego level, because it's not aligned with ego. It is something internal that transcends any external narrative telling us how we *should* be or what we *should* do.

To be compassionate is to set yourself aside for a moment and be present to what is going on, then to decide, from that place, to help or to care. The reason the two can look similar is because when someone says "have a little compassion," what they are really saying is, "please care." The same is true for "have pity." Both are an invitation to care, which means that the main difference between compassion and pity is in the intention behind how you choose to show up.

Just like the difference between empathy and sympathy, the underlying presence and awareness you bring to the situation is key. Yes, both may result in someone receiving help who needs it, which means both are an option you can choose. However, true compassion will always come from a more altruistic place—one that doesn't involve imposing any aspect of your opinion, beliefs, or desires on another living being.

So, when we talk about compassion, what we are talking about, at its core, is presence.

Who Do We See As Compassionate?

"Compassion. It's not just a word. It's a way of being. It's not just a concept. It's love in action."

– Jeff Brown

There are obvious people that we typically label as "compassionate." This often includes: caregivers, helping professionals, fundraisers and philanthropists, and volunteers, to name a few. In their various roles, they are often responsible for the well-being of another person or group.

Many in this group who take on the role through their profession see it as a vocation or calling. While others, such as volunteers, find a sense of purpose in showing up and helping out. This reinforces the notion of humans being hardwired to be part of something and to connect with others.

But who else regularly displays compassion and why (or how) do we come to label their behavior as compassionate? Firstly, let's look at some of the qualities of being compassionate. They can include being:

- Kind
- Engaged or invested
- Thoughtful
- Helpful
- Emotionally intelligent
- Resourceful (more on this in a moment)

This list is not exhaustive and you can add your own words based on your experience. In fact, it would be a good idea for you to know what your list looks like. So, please go ahead and make one.

The first five items on the list are probably obvious, but it's the 6th item that we need to take a moment to address. Resourcefulness is a common attribute of compassionate people. This means that they have the ability to bring certain things to any situation, and, perhaps more importantly, they think about what resources they have. In the sympathy/empathy example we used earlier, the resourcefulness included a ladder to be able to climb out of the hole (alone, if necessary).

Resourcefulness, therefore, is more than just financial, though many primarily think of it in that way. Instead, I would invite you to think about it as a form of mindful knowing, because resourcefulness is about *all* the things you have that can help in any given situation. Among other things, this can include your experience, connections, emotional tools (calm, humor, vulnerability), and time. In other words, when it comes to compassion, resourcefulness is also about presence.

There are some individuals that exhibit natural compassion through the presence they bring to any situation. We know it when we see it. It transcends basic caring and kindness; it's something more. Interestingly, young children often have this level of compassion before they learn otherwise. Their world of constant learning and growing naturally requires them to be present almost all the time. They bring intense focus to almost everything they do. Think of the last time you watched a 2-year-old stare at a butterfly. It's highly likely that they want nothing more than to connect with the butterfly as they watch it in awe. They don't want to kill it, control it, or otherwise impose on it; they want to relate to it, hold it, touch it. They want to understand it. The presence they bring allows them to feel compassion for another living thing. Of course, this is temporary, as something else will inevitably excite their attention, but for that moment, the attention they are giving an insect can be viewed as compassionate.

They can also do this with humans, especially other children. There are numerous videos online that show interviews with toddlers and pre-schoolers naturally moving to hug another who is sad, or holding hands when someone seems scared. Of course, it's not *all* children, and of course situations can change this behavior, but in general, if you allow a child to be a child, many will display compassion naturally.

Why? Because at the end of the day, it is in our nature for all humans to be compassionate. *All* of us. We are born with compassion on board so that we can connect with others; it's part of our survival, remember.

Unfortunately, by the time we are adults, many of us have been taught that compassion is a form of weakness or that it could be detrimental to our own situation and circumstance. A continual message of lack has created a situation where we fear losing out if we share our resources, whatever they may be. This virus of an idea that life is limited in this way has meant that we have lost much of the one thing that makes life worthwhile: Connection.

Compassion will always result in more connection, not less. When we see a compassionate person, there's a part of us that remembers that... and probably longs for more of it. So, when we ask who do we see as compassionate, we ought to add a second question: Do you see yourself as compassionate?

How Can We Learn Compassion?

"When you have learned compassion for yourself, compassion for others is automatic."

– Henepola Gunaratana

As we just discussed, compassion is natural for most people but can get pushed aside for other pursuits somewhere along the way, usually in early adulthood. The resulting impact is multi-layered and far-reaching, including everything from the planet down to us as individuals. In short, everything has suffered from the decrease in compassion. It may seem subtle, but the decline is anything but small and nuanced... once you add the element of time. So, let's back up for a second.

If we look at indigenous cultures around the world, it wouldn't be a stretch to say that most live in compassionate coexistence with their environment. They use what they need and not more. Their society is not based on consumption, it's based on balance. They know that if they exhaust their resources, they, themselves, will eventually suffer. Of course, there are modern exceptions to this, but in general, it's been their truth for millennia.

It was also the truth for many non-indigenous cultures and peoples around the world up until the industrial revolution and beyond. Though there are still communities who practice subsistence living today (and more are starting to embrace this way of life), in general, consumption is how many of us live, especially in the West. We consume more than we need, because we live in a space of chronic desire—the result of the messages of lack.

We also live in constant aspiration, or striving. There are many reasons for this, but that could be an entire book unto itself. Suffice to say that aspirational messaging (and the promises it offers, but rarely keeps) has resulted in societies around the world burning through resources at unprecedented levels. This has led to disconnection from the planet, each other, and, actually, ourselves. The result? We are living less compassionate lives in less compassionate societies.

But all is not lost. We can learn compassion. Or, perhaps better stated, we can remember compassion. We can actively pursue a life with more connection, balance, inner joy, and peace—because compassion has all that to offer, and more. So, how do we do it?

If you feel that you are compassionate already, but would like to increase it, this is for you. If you feel you aren't as compassionate as you would like, this is for you. If you fear you aren't compassionate or have forgotten how to be, this is for you. Even if you know you are compassionate, this is for you. Everyone can benefit from being more compassionate, and the world benefits from all of us showing up with more compassion. Here's how to go about it:

1. **Focus** — Identify something or someone that you can relate to. This can be a program, a person, an organization, an environment, or almost anything else. The key here is that you can relate to it/them on some level. For example, if you lost a parent to cancer when you were very young, you might identify children in similar circumstances as a group you'd like to connect with and help.

2. **Assess** — Identify what needs this person or group might have that are missing or diminished, then identify what resources you have that might help to fill that gap. Be realistic. You cannot give more than you have, nor can you give all that you have. If you deplete yourself it's of no benefit to anyone.

3. **Connect** — Find the necessary routes for connection. Look for online groups or local organizations. If you want to support a community, look for opportunities that are group-oriented. If you want to support an individual, look for one-on-one, sponsor-sponsee, or mentoring relationship opportunities.

4. **Engage** — Make your plan to get involved and do it. This should include understanding what level of commitment you can make. Then take that step into compassion and connection.

This acronym (FACE) is deliberate, because ultimately what you're doing is facing your own humanity. Your desire to (re)learn compassion is about becoming more human, more connected, and part of a solution to many of the chronic issues we face in the world. When you take the time to look in the mirror and ask yourself what you can do, you are laying the first stone in the path back to who you are at your core as a naturally compassionate living being.

The short version of all this is: Compassion is *remembered* through action. While you can teach people to be kind, thoughtful, or caring, compassion is something more. It's a state of being and something we all have access to—we just have to wake it up! Taking action is the best (and possibly only) way to get back to being compassionate. The even better news is that it's self-reinforcing. Once you engage with being more compassionate, you remember how it feels and it's easier to keep going.

Just remember that compassion doesn't exist solely in big gestures. It can be a hug at the end of a long day or rescuing a bee from almost drowning in a water bucket. It can be as simple as giving a bottle of water to an unhoused person or volunteering to mentor a child who is struggling in school. It can be many different things in a day; in fact, once you start engaging with life this way, it probably will be. The opportunities are almost infinite.

The Benefits of Compassion

"If we want to create a viable, peaceful world, we've got to integrate compassion into the gritty realities of 21ˢᵗ century life."

– Karen Armstrong

Once you've started engaging with compassion on a regular basis, you might wonder what it's really doing. You likely already feel better being more compassionate and you know that it's helping others, as well. But what else can it do?

We have discussed many of the effects being more compassionate can create, including the impact it can have on communities, societies, and environments. What we haven't discussed is how being more compassionate—that is, engaging in compassionate behaviors—can impact your inner world. In this scenario, "inner world" refers to both your personal/core relationships with others, as well as your internal psyche and body.

For your core relationships, there are some very specific benefits. When you are more compassionate, you have more patience and possibly more tolerance. This does not mean that you are a doormat allowing others to walk all over you; you still need to have strong boundaries. It just means that your reactivity is decreased. You are less likely to be reactive when you practice compassion in your relationships.

A real-life example of this may look like being tired at the end of the day and wanting to sit quietly while reading or watching a program on TV while the person next to you (a child, partner, roommate/friend) needs to share a story. Their day was eventful and they are trying to process what happened through sharing. If you can take perspective and see that their need is 1) urgent or time-sensitive (for them), and 2) temporary, you might choose to delay your quiet time in order to show up for them for a few minutes. Keeping boundaries, you could say, "I see you need to talk about this. How about we pause the movie for a bit so you can share, and then we can both watch it, together?"

A Note About Boundaries

Boundaries do not need to be mean or harsh to be maintained, though they do need to be firm. There are many ways you can practice compassion in your relationships while maintaining boundaries. One of my favorite ways to do this is to simply ask: "What do you need from me at this moment?"

I then get to assess whether or not I can meet their needs once they've stated them (and if they're realistic). If I can, I will do my best to help. If I can't, I will suggest something else within my resources. Not only does this allow me to keep my boundaries, it also prompts the other person to pause and think more clearly about what they are actually asking/feeling/doing. Though it can feel uncomfortable at first, this approach creates healthier relationships in the long run.

These types of exchanges often lead to stronger and healthier relationships, which is a wonderful benefit to practicing more compassion in your inner world. But there's another benefit that happens more internally and it's one that fuels itself, seemingly forever.

Being compassionate can create a cyclical cause-and-effect loop in your entire being. In other words, each compassionate action invites you to make another compassionate action as your inner self remembers this way of being. It becomes self-reinforcing. The feel-good chemicals that permeate your body can't help but invite you to do more.

Compassion, therefore, may be addictive, but in the best possible way. And while you may first be engaging in compassionate behavior because it makes you feel better, you will soon come to find that it's easier than *not* engaging in compassion.

It's easier to be kind, thoughtful, and caring than it is to be cruel, hurtful, and disparaging. The latter are low-frequency emotions, which means they need to continuously be re-upped or reinforced in order to be maintained. They take effort, and ultimately, if they don't take effort, it's because you may have transformed your natural state of being into one that is aligned with fear, disconnection, and even hatred. *Yikes!*

If you want to create a better life for yourself and for others, the way forward is through compassion. If you want to feel better, the best remedy is compassion. If you want to make the world a better place, it starts with compassion.

A Story About Self-Reinforcing Compassion

Years ago, I met an environmentalist who is passionate about the bug world—admittedly, something I was not. However, a couple years before I met him, I remember spending one afternoon watching "bugs" go about their daily life. Specifically, I watched ants for hours go in and out of their ant holes with food and other items. Selfishly, I found it to be very meditative; I certainly wasn't doing it for their well-being.

However, as I watched the ants, I naturally started to take perspective. I asked myself what the ants must think of me. I am a giant in their world, but am I a threat? Perhaps. I didn't know. Just asking questions, though, was enough to get me to start thinking more compassionately about insects. Then I met the environmentalist.

Through our conversations, I found myself intrigued by his passion for this category of species

---

that we, as humans, have a tendency to kill any chance we can get. While I have no intention of holding millipedes in my hand like he does, I do "rescue" spiders from my home and transfer them outside. By taking perspective and making connections, I have tapped into compassion for another living being that previously scared me. This is the life-giving power of compassion. (Quite literally, for the spiders.)

What If I'm Struggling?

"Depression taught me the importance of compassion and hard work, and that you can overcome enormous obstacles."

– Rob Delaney

To struggle is part of the human condition. In my experience, there is not a single person on the planet that hasn't experienced some level of struggle. The difference from one person to another resides in the aspects and intensity of the struggle. For example, some may struggle with mental health while being physically healthy and strong. Someone else may struggle financially, while having great mental health. The variety of struggles humans can experience sometimes feels like a never-ending list.

In short, everyone struggles.

At some point in your life, if you are struggling, you may find yourself feeling resentful and think: "But, who's helping *me?*" This is especially true if someone suggests you be compassionate toward others while undergoing your own challenges. This is normal. When we are struggling with something, we are often living in the flight-fight-freeze space in our brain—the part of the brain associated with basic survival instincts. This means it can be incredibly hard to access the places in our brains that invite connection, such as compassion. So, what do we do?

When this occurs, it's time to go back to basics. If you are struggling, you probably need compassion from others. In the same way that the compassion we practice creates connection for us, we can reverse engineer the process and use connection to receive compassion during a time of need. Therefore, when we are struggling, the single-most important thing we can do is choose connection. Almost all types of struggle will be improved or lessened by engaging in connection with others.

This is why process groups (like grief groups or AA) can be incredibly helpful. It's also why finding and creating various points of connection throughout your life is important. For example, if you are already connected, your group will probably see you struggling and reach out to engage with you before you are able to take action yourself. This type of connection used to be natural, ages ago when we lived in small, tribal communities. The tribe knew that healthy individuals meant a healthy community. They knew that everyone in the group needed to be supported, and not through mandates or obedience, but through compassion and connection.

Therefore, when you're doing well, it's even more important to be compassionate, because compassion creates connection. And when you're struggling, that connection can result in receiving compassion when you need it most.

Why Do We Need Compassion?

"Spirituality is allowing compassion and love to flourish. When belongness begins, corruption ends."

– Sri Sri Ravi Shankar

There are so many reasons we have already discussed as to why we need compassion. From our basic well-being to the health of the planet as a whole, compassion can make everything better for everyone. It's the ultimate "rising tide" example, as in: A rising tide lifts all boats. The tide doesn't judge or choose, it simply does what it's meant to do as it rises and falls. It doesn't deem one boat more or less worthy than another. It simply shows up and makes sailing possible for every boat in the water.

Compassion does the same thing. Having a more compassionate society can lead to a more balanced (presumably better) world. The ancient Greek philosophers discussed this over 2,000 years ago with both Aristotle (384–322 B.C.E.) and Epicurus (341–270 B.C.E.) offering helpful perspectives on the subject:

> **Aristotle** – Though he didn't use the word "compassion" directly, he suggested that compassion and indignation are two opposing reactions to imbalance; one to undeserved suffering and the other to undeserved good fortune.

> **Epicurus** – With his focus on the great importance of friendship, he believed that acting with compassion brought forth the greatest pleasure in these relationships.

If we are to take these two perspectives to heart, the core of compassion resides in action, both proactive and reactive. If it is not action to relieve suffering (reactive), it is action taken to increase connection (proactive). When both are practiced, life cannot help but be improved.

As if to help us on our way to living with more compassion, we can break these approaches down even further by addressing when we need to practice compassion the most:

- Daily

- In crisis

In our daily lives, practicing compassion with one another and via our special interests (like volunteering) is healthy. It leads to a better state of mental and emotional well-being. It's a proactive (maintenance and development) approach to compassion that brings multiple benefits both to us and to our communities. Like toppings on a sundae, it just makes everything a little sweeter.

When we are in crisis, however, compassion is a must. It's not the toppings or the ice cream, it's the bowl. Without compassion, very little can happen without potentially causing more mess. When we are in crisis, we need compassion like we need air or water. Ultimately, we may need compassion from ourselves, but to get through the crisis, we most likely need it from others first. Their compassion gives us the support and understanding we need to create mental-emotional (and sometimes physical) space. Crises take up an inordinate amount of space in our minds when we are going through them. Having someone help relieve some of the burden can make all the difference.

Similarly, when someone else is in crisis, we get to draw on our resources and offer compassion, especially if we are practicing compassion on a daily basis. This can be a life-affirming response both for them and for us. Compassion can also be easier to offer when we are practicing it regularly.

When we practice compassion in our everyday life, we *become* more compassionate. When we are more compassionate, we give more compassion to others. It really is that simple.

If you want to live a better life, compassion needs to be part of the equation. More compassion leads to a healthier, more balanced, happier, well-lived life... a life you can look back on with joy, gratitude, and peace.

Conclusion

"I don't really think about doing something kind, I think there's just a way to conduct your daily life with compassion to other people."

– Kat Dennings

Practiced in both words and actions, compassion means to

- Speak kindly with respect, patience, and candor.
- Act thoughtfully with consideration, caring, and acceptance.

True compassion is a healthy undertaking that leads to multiple benefits with no negative side effects (if you remember to have boundaries). Anyone and everyone can benefit from more compassion. It is said that human beings have only exercised a small fraction of their potential. When you choose compassion as part of your life, you are aligning with more of the full potential of both the planet and being human.

Compassion is not weakness, nor is it a path to accepting bad (or self-detrimental) behavior. Instead, think of compassion as a superpower—one that means you are more evolved emotionally and ready for what's to come. Being compassionate means that you recognize that you are a part of something greater, whether you consider that to be your community, society, or even the earth and all her species, as a whole.

To be compassionate takes inner strength. It takes clarity of mind and purpose. It takes a belief in something "more" and knowing that together we can help to create that "more"—whatever that may be. It honors the truth that we are all connected and creates a pathway for connection.

UNDERSTANDING
ENERGY

"Your energy introduces you even before you speak."

Unknown

Introduction

"If you want to find the secret of the universe, think in terms of energy, frequency, and vibration."

– Nikola Tesla

"Energy" is a word that gets used (and misused) almost to excess in today's world. It represents a whole host of things from people's emotions to mysterious forces at work behind some sort of wizardly curtain. It's both tangible and intangible in how we apply it and understand it, which has opened it up to a lot of interpretation—and misinterpretation.

The truth is that energy is much simpler, cleaner, and more specific than our common usage of the word implies. As such, it also can become a bit more complex to understand when we strip away all the things it's not to land on what it actually is. That is because it's essentially a tangible intangible. Energy simply is, while also being something we can't really quantify. Not yet, at least.

So, what is energy? What does it do, or not do? How does it impact our lives? How can we impact it? And, perhaps more importantly, why does it matter that you understand all this?

Let's dive in!

What Is Energy?

"What is this, that I have, that is not nothing?"

– William Shakespeare

Energy is everything and nothing at exactly the same time. Everything is made up of energy. Literally, everything. The boulder sitting idle on the side of the road? The flower blooming at night? The bird flying overhead and the waterfall? They're all made up of energy. Similarly, you, your friends and family, your pets, and every stranger you meet is made up of energy.

Everything is energy.

Now, let's take it a step further. There are two kinds of energy… yes, just two. At any given moment, all energy is either active or inactive. Energy that is active is called kinetic energy, whereas energy that is dormant is called potential energy. Everything you see—and even things you can't see—are always in one of these two states. When you understand the simplicity of this, it makes it easier to know how and when you can interact with energy.

To reiterate: Potential energy and kinetic energy are the two states of energy, which is one thing. This is why energy is everything and nothing. To learn how we can intentionally interact with energy, we turn to a famous line from *Star Wars:* "Use the force, Luke."

In that moment, Luke was invited to remember that everything around him is made of energy, and that he (also being made of energy) can tap into that level of being and move with it, interacting with everything around him—both the seen and unseen, the active and the dormant.

So, in many ways, understanding energy is a way of actually developing a better understanding of our environment and the life around us—including how we interact with it. We all have an impact, whether we acknowledge it or not. Everything you do will in some way affect everything around you. The impact does not have to be monumental to be felt or to move energy. In fact, it's often the subtle little things that can move energy the most.

For example, have you ever been in the presence of someone meditating? They aren't doing anything that you can see, just sitting there quietly, and yet their presence is directly impacting everything around them. Their "energy" is having an effect on all of the energy in their environment, and vice versa. Energy always is, therefore there is no way you can't be impacting your environment, from an energetic perspective. Nor is it possible for your environment to *not* be impacting you. From an energy perspective, there is no separateness.

As such, perhaps the most tangible way to explain energy is to see it as a means by which you can begin to connect with your environment and your life in a more grounded, holistic, broader, and deeper capacity. Since energy is everywhere all the time—and you are made of energy—this perspective is what will actually help you to work with it in a more meaningful way.

Who Practices Energy Work?

"In every culture and in every medical tradition before ours, healing was accomplished by moving energy."

– Albert Szent-Györgyi

Throughout history, there have been energy workers, energy healers, and energy practitioners, in some form or another. Depending on the culture, religion, region of the world, and period of history, we have called them everything from: priests, priestesses, shamans, medicine women, medicine men, monks, oracles, and so much more. Though their practices may be different, at their core, they're all the same... so take your pick. When it comes to understanding energy, all of these titles are essentially interchangeable.

Unfortunately, we have had so many different names for energy workers that the labels we have given them actually ended up creating divisions and hierarchies, which undermines the simplest truth about energy work: It is a universal way in which we can understand the world around us better and interact and engage with it on a more holistic level.

At the end of the day, all the labels and names are a human construct and primarily serve to create a common language for ease of communicating with one another across barriers. But they can also detract from the ultimate goal of understanding energy. When you truly understand energy, you know its purpose is simple and completely devoid of any human value system. Energy simply is.

Working with energy is a tool we can use to achieve greater alignment, greater evolution, more growth, better well-being, better understanding, better connection, and all the things we hope for from a soul perspective. Idealistic? Perhaps, but no less true. If you take a moment to look at nature, when left alone, it works in harmony. Each aspect has a role and each role is carried out in balance with everything else. This is a perfect visual and tangible representation of energy. When things are balanced and harmonious, that is energy at work in its most natural state, as both kinetic and potential energy. In this way, Nature is an "energy worker" at its heart.

So, what humans practice energy? (Or who should?)

At this point in our human timeline, there are many (many!) people practicing energy. We see energy practitioners working in different paradigms, using different practices and tools. Unfortunately, we also see numerous interpretations coming forward and being marketed as being "better" than anything that came before. This undermines the nature of energy by creating the aforementioned value-driven and human-made hierarchy.

To be clear, energy has no hierarchy. Is there one method or interpretation that is better than another? No. There may be a practice or tradition that is better *for you,* but that does not mean it's better than any other modality of energy work. There is no "better" or "worse" when it comes to energy. Energy can't be pigeonholed that way, because to do so limits it, and energy has no limits. Remember, it only has two states: kinetic or potential. It cannot be more or less than that.

This leads us to another simple truth about energy, and more specifically the practice of energy work, which is this: If someone says there is only *one way* to practice or engage with energy work, you should walk away. Because this is simply not true. When it comes to energy work, there are potentially millions of ways to engage in the work. The question should be: What is the best way *for you* to practice energy work? The answer will be based on your resources, your environment, your personal values, and your soul's path.

Though there are many different ways to practice energy work, just as there are even more energy practitioners in the world, there is still only one way to truly *understand* energy, which is that it is everything and nothing at the same time. It is active and inactive and it neither dies nor is created. Energy simply is, and nothing— and nobody—can change that.

When Does Energy Matter?

"If you don't take responsibility for programming your-self, then someone else will."

– Paul McKenna

Energy matters every day of your life, whether you practice it and/or understand it, or not. The simple reason for this is twofold: 1) everything is energy, so there's no escaping it or opting out, and 2) energy is a means by which you can understand life better. It's the second piece that makes energy matter the most, because when you accept that truth, you can create a cheat sheet to life and make it easier for yourself and others.

Energy is a way to understand—and interact with—your environment better. It's a filter you can use to help you engage with life differently—usually for the better. For example, many of us have experienced being at an event when a certain person walks in, and suddenly, the entire energy of the room is either lifted or dropped. Their presence directly impacted the energy of the room, just by showing up.

This is why understanding energy matters.

How you show up in your daily life is entirely up to you and you are responsible for the energy you bring into a room. Conversely, you are *not* responsible for anybody else's energy. In that instance, you are only responsible for how you interact with or react to somebody else's energy.

So, if you are the person who is bringing a room down (or lifting a room up), that is your responsibility. Nobody else is responsible for causing, fixing, or changing that for you. Furthermore, everyone else in the room gets to react in whatever way they wish; that is their prerogative and responsibility. This is true every day of your life, for everything you do, everywhere you do it. Energy matters everywhere, all the time.

Understanding how you show up as energy may give you a greater sense of responsibility (and accountability), but it can also give you a greater sense of empowerment. That empowerment can lead to stronger boundaries and a stronger presence, including where you are willing to put your attention, because focus is a form of energy.

When you focus on something, you are essentially saying, "This is where I want to put my energy." This includes:

- When and where you are willing to show up
- What you are willing to support
- Who you are willing to be around

All of these items are a choice that you get to make when you understand energy and accept that it matters… in everything.

Where Can We Learn Energy Work?

"To heal is to touch with love that which we previously touched with fear."

– Stephen Levine

As you may now know, there are many different practices when it comes to energy work. There are even more people who teach these energy work practices, resulting in an increasing number of paradigms (or interpretations) of energy work practices. Remember: There is no "one way" or "one correct way" to study energy work. There is only what's best for you. This means it is incumbent upon you to do your due diligence when researching energy work practices and practitioners.

When doing your research, here are just a few of the questions you might want to ask:

- Where do they come from? What practice lineage and perspective?
- What do they believe? Personally and professionally?
- What have others said about them?
- Do they allow people to come and go from their practice?
- Do their teachings align with my values and beliefs?
- Can I afford this program? What are my resources?
- Do I feel any hesitancy?

That last question is very important—perhaps the most important, actually. If you feel hesitancy because you're not sure if you *really* want to study energy work, that's different. But if you feel hesitant about a practitioner—whether you are studying with them or receiving energy work from them—step away. Why? Because *you* are energy.

Even if you haven't studied yet, if you get a feeling of hesitancy, that means you are experiencing something on an energetic level, and it's always best to heed the message, even if you don't understand it. This would be akin to having a "gut feeling" about someone or something. Listen to your gut… and not just when you're hungry.

In some ways, when you study energy work with someone, you are agreeing to the energetic presence that they bring as well as the beliefs that they hold, even temporarily. So, it is your job and responsibility to really scratch beneath the surface and understand whether or not the practitioner is the right fit for you and where you are in your soul's evolution. If someone is not the right fit today, they could be the right fit next year. What matters is that you listen to your intuition (which is a form of energy) while also doing your homework and researching everything.

In this world, there are many opportunities to learn how to work with energy—making even more reasons for you to do your due diligence. Unfortunately, just as there are wonderful practitioners, there are also charlatans.

Understanding How to Spot a Charlatan

Every industry seems to have charlatans these days. What is a charlatan? The simple answer is that it's like a cross between an impostor and a conman. They serve to con you out of your money, energy (many are "energy vampires"), and other resources, while they purport to be something they are not, often in the guise of wanting to help. They may even believe the lies they are telling and selling, which can make it harder to discern.

Today, there seem to be more charlatans at work every day. Unfortunately, when it comes to energy work, the world is rife with them, and most people who are just beginning to work with energy don't yet have the tools to discern who is real and who isn't. Of course, there are a few ways you can spot a charlatan when it comes to energy work, they include:

- **Aspirational Language** – If the promises seem too good to be true, they probably are. Ask more questions, read independent reviews (not testimonials on their website), and check in on your own needs and emotions. If you are feeling desperate for a cure or some healing, you are more susceptible to charlatans who make big promises. Desperation gives off a vibe that makes you an attractive target.

- **Minimal Requirement** – If the course of work can be achieved simply and quickly, it's probably not a course you want to take. (For example, *full* certification in a weekend is probably a warning sign, as most energy practices require a lot more study and practice. Additionally, certification online or virtually should also be a red flag, as introductory energy work often requires in-person experience.)

One of the ways to think about it is this: Energy work involves impacting someone else's life. If the path to certification (or even a basic understanding) is too fast, what are you really learning? **Energy work isn't benign.** You aren't painting a wall that can be repainted; you are dealing with someone's life. The bar for entry, by design, should be higher than most. You wouldn't have surgery by someone who only took a weekend course over the internet, so please look at energy work in a similar way.

- **Fixed Thinking** – If the practitioner says their way is the "only" or "best" way, walk away. Yes, there is marketing, but there is also an inflated sense of self and belief in one's own skills and role on this planet. When a practitioner has given themselves over to ego, it's usually a sign to step away. There will be somebody else you can learn from.

- **Urgency** – If the messaging to sign up has a level of urgency and crisis or danger attached to it, this is manipulative and is definitely not aligned with the universal premise behind energy work. Energy is a constant, therefore there is never any urgency to it. Manipulation is nuanced and can come in many forms—urgency is just one. If there is manipulative language, reconsider studying with this person. (Hint: This is also a good way to spot a scam in general, since a lot of them use urgency as a way to pressure people into signing up or buying whatever they're peddling.)

Charlatans are well-versed in the language of manipulation. They often create an unspoken need or fear, which then prompts an emotion in you, for which they (conveniently) offer a solution. Again, if you come to your search feeling desperate, you are an easy target for these types of people. If you come to your search feeling balanced, and the messaging sparks desperation or urgency in you, you also become a target.

The best way to find the right practitioner or practice is to do so when you are feeling rested, well-fed, hydrated, and balanced within yourself. You are more vulnerable to charlatans when you are feeling desperate, tired, overwhelmed, or overwrought. If you feel any of those things, it's time to engage in some self-care so that you can do your research from a better place.

At the end of the day, you can learn about energy work from many different people, in many different ways and places. What matters most is that you do your research and find a place to start that feels good in your body and soul... from your heart all the way down to your toes! When it feels good, it's probably a good fit. When the feeling changes, it's probably time to move on to a new teacher. Good teachers understand this and welcome it; they even encourage it. Conversely, the teacher that wants to keep you attached to them forever is probably the one you most need to step away from.

Why Do We Need To Understand Energy Work?

"Life begets life. Energy creates energy. It is by spending oneself that one becomes rich."

– Sarah Bernhardt

As the planet is evolving—as our species is evolving—we actually need to put an effort into understanding energy work a lot more today than we used to. Over centuries, especially the last century, we have abandoned a lot of the knowledge we once held as a collective. Of course, there are still many that hold this wisdom, but we are losing it at a rapid rate.

Think of the timeline for humanity. For thousands of years, knowing how to live with nature used to be part of our inherent understanding of life. We used to know that the timing of nature served a purpose for our bodies and our minds. We knew how to work in conjunction with seasons, weather, and wildlife, and this information was passed down from one generation to the next, almost effortlessly through story and practice. Now, in the short span of just 100–200 years, we have gone away from most of the wisdom that we held for millennia as a human species.

It is important that we get back to understanding energy work because we *are* energy! We are not outside the system, we are in the system, part of the system, and we interact with the system on a daily basis. We have to understand it so that we can a) show up as our best selves in the system, and b) interact with the system appropriately.

We need to remember that everything we do has a ripple effect within the system, just as everything in the system has a ripple effect that touches us. So, it is very, very important for us to get back to a place where we understand that we are part of—not apart from—the system of energy, because we are energy ourselves.

Advancement and technology are great achievements, and in many ways, they have made life much easier on the planet for humans. But they are not the *only* way to live, nor should they be. The mistake most often made is assuming that it's an either/or choice. It's not. It's about both/and.

- We can practice energy work and engage in good uses of technology.

- We can understand our role in the larger system and still use our technological advances to offer inventions and interventions that save and/or improve lives.

It's never been about choosing one over the other; it's about learning how to incorporate both so that they complement each other and we can be better, overall. When we understand energy work from this perspective, we set ourselves—and all of the planet—up for success. We can make decisions from a place of balance and consideration, rather than from a place of false expectations and urgency. Energy work is like those two or three puzzle pieces that fell under the sofa that have prevented us from completing the picture. When we dig them out from resting among the dust bunnies, clean them off, and put them in their proper place, we can finally see what's possible and have a clearer path forward.

How Do We Work Best With Energy Systems?

"Energy can't be created or destroyed, and energy flows. It must be in a direction, with some kind of internal, emotive, spiritual direction."

– Keanu Reeves

Firstly, working with energy systems requires the due diligence we discussed previously. By conducting your research to know which protocol or method works best for you, you will be better able to truly engage with energy work when you begin. Being in alignment is an important piece of energy work, and since there are so many different practices available for study, knowing what will work best for you is the only way to begin.

Beyond that, however, we also need to consider vibration and frequency. This is true both for what you want to study, as well as for working within the energy systems in the body, within nature, and on the planet. As everything is energy, it's only logical that there are different energetic systems that help to coordinate it all.

Let's start by breaking down "vibration" and "frequency" in easy to understand language.

Vibration vs. Frequency

The best way to explain the difference between vibration and frequency is by thinking of energy as a radio station. The radio station's signal is the vibration. It transmits at this specific number on the dial that people can tune into. Then, once you've tuned in, you control the frequency, which is like the volume knob. How high or low the vibration resonates is in part controlled by you and how you choose to interact with it. Each and every radio station (vibration) can be interacted with at both high and low volumes (frequencies). You control one aspect, and the energy systems control the other.

When you can identify both vibration and frequency, you can show up more consciously with more presence. This results in greater feelings of empowerment which then invites you to engage with the world on a much more holistic basis.

The question of how to work best with energy systems takes vibration and frequency into account. When you understand how to interact with the energy system and are mindful of its nuances, you can participate in it appropriately. As we are all energy, and all part of the energy systems of the planet, we are all participating in all the systems every day. The question of whether we are participating appropriately—or consciously—is what we need to focus on.

Think of a spider's web. One of the ways a spider knows it has trapped its next meal is because the web has vibrated from touch. This is not enough, however. If a human touches a spider's web, the spider doesn't come running out with a bib under its chin, knife and fork at the ready. The specific frequency of the vibration matters. The spider has learned which prey makes which frequency, and it knows when and how to act as a result.

Now think of the energy systems of the planet as different strands in the web. Though each web is its own thing, they are all connected. A vibration on one strand will vibrate on all the other strands. When we touch the web—when we do something, consciously or not—we are affecting the whole web. Everything we do, no matter how small or big, in some way affects the whole.

We work best with all of the various energy systems when we remember this truth and take responsibility for our own energy—both the vibration and frequency at which we engage with life. While we can choose to stay within one or two energetic systems on the planet, we cannot forget that all of the systems are connected. For example, a wildlife conservationist might stay within the energy systems that are more nature-aligned. As a result, their own pace and focus might be different. But, if they were to stay there all the time, they would be completely incapacitated when they got on a plane or public transportation. Their personal system wouldn't be able to handle it if they didn't adjust to this different energy system.

When it comes to energy, being adaptable is just as important as understanding vibration and frequency so that you can adapt. It's also important to know when and how you can impact an energy system for the better. This is how we can work best with energy systems.

When Does Energy Change?

"Inner peace begins the moment you choose not to allow another person or event to control your emotions."

– Pema Chödrön

Now that we understand energy systems, it's also important to look at how energy can change within our own system, as well as what can impact our system and create change. Change is a constant and should always be expected on some level, so learning how to navigate change in relation to your own energy is important. But what creates change? Literally, anything.

Energy Change-Makers

Firstly, we need to differentiate between our environment and ourselves, that means that we have two types of stimulus that can create change: external and internal. External stimuli can be anything in your environment from the weather to someone's bad mood. Conversely, internal stimuli are usually less tangible, like chronic self-deprecating thoughts, constant emotional processing, or overconsumption of media. However, it can also be something more tangible and simple like getting a cold or the flu.

Regardless of whether the cause is internal or external, both will impact our energy in some way. Similarly, the stimulus can be both good and less-good. It's not just about being affected negatively, it can also be about being impacted positively by something. For example, someone else's good mood at the result of a promotion at work can give us a boost of adrenaline and joy as we share in the happy energetic waves they are sending out. It can also follow that an hour or two later, we find ourselves crashing because of the removal of the same stimulus.

In short, anything and everything can affect and impact our energy, whether it's "good" or "bad" in essence. If you are alive and living in the world, your energy will be impacted by the world around you as well as how you process it. There is no way to escape this, nor should you want to. It's what makes you human and what makes life engaging. The goal, therefore, is to learn how to ride these waves with grace and ease by creating your own energetic surfboard.

Riding the Waves of Change

When change occurs within our own energy system, it can feel unsettling regardless of where it comes from—especially if we are used to having things be in balance. This type of shift requires some introspection followed by tools that can help us regain our footing. Most of the tools we would use can be filed under "self-care" and might include:

- Pampering (aromatherapy baths, facials, saunas, massage)
- Down time (meditation, naps, gentle walks in nature)
- Nourishment (healthy and/or comforting food and good hydration)
- Reflection (reading, journaling, therapy, calling a friend)

Understanding what works best for you will help you create a shortlist that you can use at any time to redirect your energy and find balance. In addition to these self-care items, you can also keep a list of time-limited interventions that will buy you a little space and time until you can get to a self-care practice. In this instance, you would choose an item based on the amount of time you have.[5] An example of this type of list can look like:

1. 0–30 seconds: A few photos of your favorite people or pets
2. 30–60 seconds: A folder of favorite memes

---

[5] Though I have been teaching this to my clients for almost two decades, in recent times, I have heard this referred to by others as a "Dopamine Menu" which is brilliant! If you want to do more research and get more examples, use that phrase.

3. 1–3 minutes: A compilation of quotes or a favorite comedian's video

4. 3+ minutes: A favorite song or a favorite video or compilation of videos

Having tools at the ready can help you reset more easily when things around you have changed and you find your energy has gone a bit wonky. Being prepared makes it easier to redirect, as you don't have to think about what you should do, you just do it. Since we can always expect change, creating these lists for yourself is a life-hack that can make everything easier.

Minimizing Change From Internal Sources

Though both internal and external stimuli can create energetic changes for us, we can be proactive about minimizing the internal events that do this. External events will almost always be outside of our control, but how we react to them or engage with them is something we get to choose. This means that we can invite ourselves to exercise a bit more influence over our own thoughts, behaviors, and emotions—or the things that make us human.

If, for example, you know that you get triggered when watching a specific show to the point that you feel deflated afterward, you might want to choose a different activity. (Yes, even if it's your roommate's favorite.) Similarly, if you know that scrolling through social media in the morning invigorates you, but scrolling at night brings you down, changing your behavior can directly change the impact on your energy.

Though both of these examples involve an external aspect, they originate with an internal decision: Where to put your attention. When you start to raise your awareness to how your internal decisions affect your thoughts and emotions, you are reclaiming your energetic power.

Doomscrolling is only "doom-related" if it makes you feel bad and detached from yourself and the world around you. Even though there are times in our life when checking out can be good for us, doing so on a regular basis is rarely a good idea. The key to all of this is understanding that it's a choice you get to make.

Just as it's a choice to reply to an angry text, an inconsiderate driver, or any other type of external event in your day, it's also a choice to react to your own internal events. The messaging you give yourself on a regular basis will always have a greater impact on your energy than anything external. As such, if you really want to ride energetic waves like a pro surfer, you will want to start with yourself and check in on the type of energy *you* are bringing to your days through the thoughts you have and the language you use. Once you've done that, you will really begin to understand how empowered you can be.

Protecting Your Energy

"Energy is contagious, positive and negative alike. I will forever be mindful of what and who I am allowing into my space."

– Alex Elle

Just as learning how to be flexible and adaptable to navigate change is important, you can also learn how to protect your energy. This section is not intended to be comprehensive, but instead to provide an overview of what's possible when it comes to energy work and creating protections. Each modality of study or tradition will have its own best practices and offer a deeper dive into the nuance of protection. Use the one that works for you.

That being said, there are certain aspects of protection that they all have in common, one of which is an understanding of what's ours—and what's not ours. This is the first step to incorporating any kind of energetic protection in your life. In fact, simply asking the question, "Is this mine?" is a good place to start.

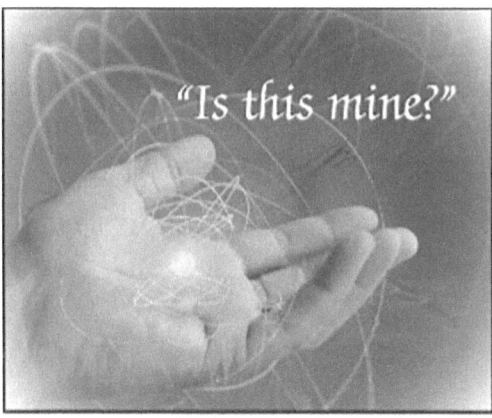

When it comes to energy, being able to discern what's yours and what's somebody else's allows you to address the situation with more clarity and choose a path forward that will be most helpful. For example, many empaths often report struggling when going into a hospital because of all the suffering going on. As such, they are often taught to protect themselves before entering the building. This is not to disparage the patients in the hospital, rather it's to keep a firm boundary between what belongs to which person. If an empath is feeling the patient's suffering in a way that they are no longer able to help, that's not good for anybody.

Similarly, you often hear of protection being needed at large family gatherings, particularly over the holidays. This is not because people are inherently "bad" or "wrong" (though it sometimes can be), but it's often because in such groups there is a lack of respect for each other's emotional boundaries. This in turn can lead to energy violations that leave people feeling upset, angry, and/or depleted. It's such a common occurrence, actually, that it's usually incorporated in modern cultural narratives like movies and TV shows. Protection, in this regard, is about both keeping energetic boundaries as well as physical/emotional ones. This can look like envisioning layers of energetic protection before ever entering the room and leaving a room before getting overwhelmed (excusing oneself to the bathroom always works).

Protecting your energy is first and foremost about connecting with yourself and knowing yourself well enough to make decisions that are in alignment with your best self. From there, you can implement a wide array of tools and exercises to move through life with more ease and less disruption.

How Can You Use Energy?

"Energy is the currency of the universe.
You get what you give."
– Oprah

Energy is everything and everything is energy. This means that you can use it all the time, if you choose. Or you can use energy in ways that are more direct and specific. It's up to you. How and when you use your knowledge of energy doesn't change the fact that it's always there. Always. In truth, however, developing an energy practice as well as an energy ethos is probably the best way to engage with energy on a regular basis.

What Is an Energy Ethos?

In this regard, an ethos is like a "guiding principle" for your life. How you choose to work with energy will likely be grounded in your beliefs about it combined with your experience of it. This will create a roadmap for you to engage with energy on a regular basis in a way that feels comfortable and allows you to grow and progress at your own pace. Understanding your energy ethos, as well as what practices and traditions align with your ethos is an important step in your journey working with energy. In order to create your energy ethos, you will need to answer a couple questions:

1. What do I want to experience with energy work and how do I want to feel about engaging with energy in a new way?

2. How do I want my new experiences to impact my life going forward?

These questions will help guide you to creating a personal relationship with energy work that comes from within you. Once you have established that, you will be better able to connect with a practice, a tradition, and/or a teacher. Your energy ethos should be grounded in your core values as well as be in alignment with your life, or the life you want to create.

What Is an Energy Practice?

Most energy work traditions incorporate some aspect of practice. This means that when you begin to study energy work, you will need to practice. You will also benefit from a system of checks and balances that will help you hone your understanding and your skills. It's always best to learn from somebody who is further along the path, as they will have information and experience to impart that can help you.

Once you have identified a tradition or a teacher to study with, you will want to create a daily practice to help you connect with and understand energy on a personal level. It's important to have a tangible personal understanding before ever moving into a profes-sional capacity. Why? Because 1) It's a good parameter to have, and 2) It's common sense. If you don't know what it feels like and can't explain what it means to you, how can someone ever trust you to help them? More importantly, though, why *should* they?

There's a saying among helping professionals that feels apt here: *Someone can only take you as far as they, themselves, have gone.* If they don't know the landscape, they will struggle to walk you through it. So, you should hold the same level of understanding for yourself, even if you don't want to become a professional energy worker and just want to learn about energy for personal use and growth.

To create a daily practice, the sky's the limit! Your practice can (and should) look like whatever will work best for you, and it can include things like:

- Meditation (guided, structured, or free)
- Movement (yoga, tai chi, forest bathing)
- Nourishment (diet can impact energy)
- Art (expressing oneself is a way to connect with energy)

- Tools (Tarot, runes, card decks, etc.)
- Free-flow writing and prompted journaling
- Specific practices based on the tradition you study

Working with energy is a gift you give to yourself, and then bring to the world. When you begin to understand the basics of how energy works—and accept that everything is energy—you can truly start to live from a different place. Not only do you feel more empowered, but from an empowered state you often take more responsibility for your own life which allows you to be more deliberate about creating a life that fulfills you. This, in some ways, is the most wonderful side effect of understanding energy: A more fulfilled life. What a gift!

Conclusion

"Energy cannot be created or destroyed; it can only be changed from one form to another."

– Albert Einstein

Whether you want to learn about energy to use it professionally or to simply create a better life for yourself and your family, the choice is yours. Ultimately, both will be of benefit to the world. More people working with energy, from a place of truly understanding what it is, can only bring about greater planetary change, for the better. Though energy work can be (and has been) misused by some people over millennia, it also holds the promise of a more beneficial future. This is because understanding energy is about understanding ourselves—who we are and who we can be.

When you understand that everything is energy, and that energy is either dormant or active, you unlock the door to living a more deliberate life. The key is accepting that working with energy creates empowerment, and empowerment creates possibility. From there, probability is the next logical step... and it all starts with you!

Working with energy is something you can learn at any age, anywhere, and create something new in your life. It changes how you interact with the world around you, usually for the better. When you understand energy, your world opens up and becomes so much bigger than anything you have experienced before. Simultaneously, it also becomes much more connected, which makes it feel somehow smaller, in the best possible ways.

UNDERSTANDING

GRATITUDE

"When I started counting my blessings,
my whole life turned around."

Willie Nelson

Introduction

"Gratitude is the fairest blossom which springs from the soul."

– Henry Ward Beecher

Gratitude is a topic that has been discussed throughout history. From philosophers to world leaders, entertainers to teachers, it feels like everyone has had an opinion and perspective to share. For example, we see gratitude tied to some measure of justice when we go all the way back to Seneca[6] and Aquinas.[7] Whereas in more recent years, Nelson Mandela defined gratitude as a "prescription" while Eckhart Tolle refers to it as a measurement of prosperity. These are all definitions that work, even though they seem different. But, why?

This is because, gratitude is, in effect, one of the simplest things we can access (even children do it without being taught), and one of the hardest things to accurately define beyond the action of saying "thank you." It is something that is often discussed, more often prescribed, and too often misunderstood or misinterpreted. Even though gratitude is universally expressed and universally understood, it's still incredibly personal.

So, what is gratitude, really? And, why do we need gratitude in our lives? Finally, how do we express gratitude? Is there a measure of gratitude that is universally accepted? All of these questions and more are the reason why we are still discussing gratitude today. Thankfully.

If you want a deeper understanding of gratitude and why creating a life that embodies gratitude is important, you will find answers in these pages. Truly understanding gratitude is about more than learning what it is; it's about knowing how to apply it in your own life to reap its many benefits. So, let's dive in.

---

[6] Circa 4 BCE–65 CE

[7] 1225–1274

What Is Gratitude?

"Gratitude is the power to connect with the cosmos and harness its energy."

– Sukant Ratnakar

Though many have defined gratitude for millennia, the definitions usually focus on the effects of gratitude or the act of gratitude, in relation to self or other. Being grateful, giving thanks, and showing appreciation are all ways we describe gratitude, and they are accurate in that they are synonyms. However, none of them actually get to the core of what gratitude really is. So, what is gratitude?

Gratitude is the feeling—and the tool—that takes you out of your head and into your heart.

"Feeling and tool" and "head to heart" are the two key aspects of that sentence. By taking a deeper dive into why these points are important, we can truly begin to understand the power and potential of gratitude—as well as its true meaning in our lives, and, more importantly, how we can best employ it. So, let's break this down a bit further.

Gratitude as a Feeling

Gratitude is a state of being more than anything else—which means it's something you have to feel. Or rather, you *get* to feel, because gratitude is a choice. Even though it is most often linked to an action (such as giving thanks or keeping a gratitude journal), ultimately, the most powerful form of gratitude occurs when it's felt. As a state of being, gratitude realizes its true potential when it is more than a phrase or an action. (Though, those are often the easiest ways we can begin to access gratitude, making them a good place to start.)

To better understand this, let's call gratitude the antidote to low frequency emotions, things like: fear, sadness, frustration, and anger. Like all good antidotes, they are most effective when applied quickly and deliberately. When our emotions develop frayed edges, gratitude becomes the balm that soothes. When we feel low, rough, or calloused, applying gratitude can help us shift out of that space and heal.

Gratitude becomes the tincture that helps to bring calm and peace to an otherwise overly active mind or body. It takes what is going on and almost alchemically transforms it into something else. In this way, gratitude is almost like magic. But, because it can be used tangibly and applied specifically, it's not magic. Instead, we can think of it as a form of medicine—one that brings focus back to the heart when we feel overwhelmed, scattered, or scared.

Gratitude as a Tool

As much as it is a state of being, gratitude is also a tool that can be used and practiced anywhere by anyone at any time for anything. This makes it universal… and incredibly powerful! As a universal tool, it is probably also the most expeditious tool we have. In other words, it can bring us back into a more peaceful and aligned state of being faster than almost anything else. Regardless of what you have going on, if you use gratitude as a tool to redirect your thoughts, it can take you out of virtually anything and help to restore balance. It does this almost instantly, too. As tools go, there are few (if any) that are faster.

Of course, there are many ways gratitude can be used as a tool, but the most commonly accepted method is probably keeping a gratitude journal. In a gratitude journal, a person typically writes down three things they are grateful for on a daily basis, often at the end of the day. By doing so, they are refocusing their thoughts to that which gives them peace, joy, or comfort and happiness before sleep. This shift in focus just before bed will serve to shift the individual's presence over time. This means that, with time, their thoughts will slowly align to ones that are more heart-centered resulting in a more peaceful life.

As a tool, a gratitude journal is a relatively simple method that is available to anyone and everyone. As long as you have a method to capture your list, whether that's with pen and paper or by typing electronically, you can keep a gratitude journal.

The Journey from Head to Heart

Now that we have differentiated between the feeling and tool aspects of gratitude, let's look at how they apply to the journey from the head to the heart. This aspect (the transfer from head to heart) in the definition for gratitude is possibly the most important. Why? Because it's ultimately what makes gratitude so powerful. It's the alchemy that gratitude gifts us, and it's potentially infinite in its application and results.

Whether felt or used as a tool, the result of being in gratitude is that your focus shifts from one that is *thinking* (and potentially over-processing) to one that is *being*. When we are living from our heart center, we are more aligned with presence than when we live from our heads. Some liken this to the "gut feeling" we can get about something, even when our head disagrees. Though we say "gut" in that phrase, it's more similar to being in our heart.

In a busy life and a busy world, we can get too easily distracted by the noise and bustling nature of things. As a result, we live in our heads more often than not, which has its benefits, but can also go awry. In our modern times, there needs to be a balance between head- and heart-centered living, and gratitude is the piece that can help to restore that balance when things have gone a bit wonky. It serves as a bridge between the two so that we can quickly and easily rebalance. We just have to remember that a) It's important to rebalance, b) It's possible to rebalance, and c) Gratitude can help us rebalance, easily.

Understanding what gratitude means in reality is the first step to transforming your life. When you have a better grasp on how it can positively affect your life, you can begin to apply it in various situations to reap its many benefits. In this way, it's also important to be authentic in your gratitude for it to work. So, let's look at what could undermine your practice of gratitude.

What Gratitude Isn't

Just as it's important to understand what gratitude is, it's also important to understand what it is not. Gratitude at its core is not about performance. When gratitude becomes performative, the lack of authenticity behind it can slowly erode trust and ultimately negatively impact relationships and circumstances.

We see this when acts of appreciation are generated automatically, such as with form letters thanking people for something. Yes, it's important to say thank you, and yes it is important to acknowledge gifts of any kind; however, when a thank you letter is generated repeatedly and automatically, without any effort to make a connection, the long-term result is usually one of disengagement. Eventually, though, that can get worse. Once they've become an expectation, if the automatic letters are removed, for example, the change in the behavioral pattern can actually damage relationships.

We also see this when the act of gratitude is imposed on someone, which makes it performative. Unless you're a child who is being taught the importance of expressing appreciation, being forced to say "thank you" or state something you're grateful for when you don't want to (or aren't feeling it) undermines any connection that could have been possible. In other words, it's not actually gratitude if you're being forced or coerced to do it.

Just as authentic gratitude isn't performative, it's also not an overture. This means that when gratitude is expected, an overture is usually made in an effort to meet expectations. This usually isn't authentic gratitude, but rather a form of appreciation. To understand the difference between gratitude and appreciation, try this exercise:

- Stand in front of the mirror and look at yourself, saying: "I appreciate you."

- Stand in front of a mirror and look at yourself, saying: "I am grateful for you."

Even if you can't put your finger on exactly why these two statements are not the same, you will probably be able to say you *felt* a difference, however small. The undertone between the two is inherently different, as it is meant to be. While both are nice, gratitude feels more profound with deeper roots than appreciation.

Appreciation is often a form of expression that is done as part of an (unspoken) agreement; whereas gratitude is an expression of something altogether more personal. Ultimately, true transformative gratitude has to be real and come from your heart to be effective.

However, to fully understand gratitude and its powerful role in our lives, we need to look at how we share it and the effect it can have, both on ourselves and on others.

How Do We Express Gratitude?

"Thanks is given in three ways: In heart, in words, and in deed."

– Thomas Aquinas

Ask anyone to define what an expression of gratitude is and you will come up with many similar answers, as well as a lot of different ones. This is because gratitude is both unique and universal. It's universal in our understanding of it when we see it in action, but it's inherently unique to each individual, as well as individual cultures, traditions, and practices.

So, how do we express gratitude? Is there a universal expression that we all understand, even one that comes from animals? And, perhaps more importantly, how do we receive gratitude? Can it ever backfire?

Giving and receiving gratitude can vary from one person to another. Understanding that simple truth is key to understanding how we express—and accept—gratitude.

Expressing Gratitude

Gratitude has a few universal expressions that seem to transcend species, such as gift-giving. For example, we have witnessed what we perceive as gratitude when a dolphin brings a sea cucumber to a human who saved his dolphin-friend from a net. We have also seen other animals express gratitude, like when a cat gives you a "present" of a dead mouse at your feet or a crow brings little "gifts" to the human that fills the bird feeder. These gifts are a form of "thank you" from one sentient being to another.

For humans, gifts can also be an expression of gratitude that crosses cultures and traditions. For example, it may be a tradition for you to bring a "hostess gift" when attending an event at someone's house as a form of gratitude. Though gifts are universally accepted as a form of gratitude, not every gift serves this purpose or sends a positive message. In fact, there are cultures in which giving certain gifts is considered bad. For example, giving someone a sharp object, such as scissors or knives, is thought to bring bad luck and represents the severing of the relationship—definitely not an ideal hostess gift (unless you're trying to send a very different message than "thank you").

As such, expressions of gratitude need to encompass more than one method (such as gift-giving), which is why it's not always easy to define. Across the world, gratitude can involve physical behaviors, such as handshakes, hugs, bows, and nods, to name a few. Alternatively, gratitude can include word-based actions, such as in letters or notes, speeches, or even multimedia messages, like memes and posts on social media.

When looked at from this perspective, the potential ways to share our gratitude with others is almost limitless. The only constraints lie in the restrictions placed upon us by our resources, social norms, rules, or traditions.

~~~~~

Thus far, the focus has been on how we express gratitude to others, but what about simply feeling gratitude in our own lives? How do we express gratitude when it isn't directed at someone else, or even something else, like an event or situation? How do we express gratitude when we are alone or within the realm of our own life? This is the type of gratitude that we will primarily focus on in this book, because this is the gratitude that can bring about the internal and external changes that we seek.

This type of gratitude is less about acts of service or gift-giving (though you can certainly reward yourself with a gift for doing something or accomplishing something). Instead, the expressions of gratitude we make to ourselves involve thoughts and feelings. They include making a deliberate choice to shift our focus and perspective to get to a different place in our minds... and our lives.

By expressing gratitude in this way, we don't have to attach it to a person or something external, though that can be the original focus. Instead, we attach gratitude to how we internalize things that are external. This means that we identify something external for which we are grateful, then bring it internally and give it meaning.

For example, if you express gratitude for air conditioning on a hot day, you may be identifying something external in your gratitude journal, but the feeling you are internalizing through this expression of gratitude—the meaning you attach to the feeling—is what matters. Do you feel relief? Do you feel comfort? Do you feel joy? Whatever it is you are feeling amplifies the gratitude resulting in more high-frequency emotions, such as love, hope, and peace.

Have you ever seen someone cry tears of joy or gratitude? This is what it means to be fully grateful in your heart. Expressing gratitude is the gateway to other heart-centered feelings that can truly transform a life.

Expressing gratitude when you are alone can be a powerful exercise, one that rewards you with a happier, more balanced, and peaceful life. To live a life of gratitude is to be in touch with your heart and make choices that reinforce that which brings you joy and makes your heart smile.

Now, how you choose to express gratitude to others is one thing; how you choose to feel grateful within your own skin is entirely up to you—and it's the tool that changes everything.

Who Benefits From Gratitude?

"The miracle of gratitude is that it shifts your perception to such an extent that it changes the world you see."

– Dr. Robert Holden

We all benefit from engaging with gratitude. As much as it helps to improve our personal situation, it also helps to improve our lives and the lives of those around us. This is primarily because of the rebalancing that happens between the head and the heart discussed previously. However, it's also because gratitude requires us to slow down a bit, which then allows us to engage more fully with life. The simple truth is: When we are less rushed, we are more present.

When we are more present, it can be easier for us to be our best selves, and we do this when we incorporate a state of gratitude into our daily life. Being your best self means being the best version of who you are, or who you can be. We are human, and it's important to remember and understand that we are always evolving and growing.

Also, as humans, we can make mistakes that cause problems and strife. We can also experience problems and strife caused by others. To expect a world without any form of struggle is to be a little bit blind to reality, for it's in the struggle that we grow the most. However, not all struggle needs to carry the same level of intensity. In fact, when we are feeling low, we can sometimes attribute a higher level of intensity to the strife than what's warranted; this is where gratitude can help.

A more grateful society creates less strife, overall, as well as *less intense* strife. A more grateful person is less likely to cause struggle for others, just as they are more likely to move through their own struggles with more ease. Intensity of the issue matters almost as much as the issue itself.

Gratitude, therefore, is one of the things that can help us experience our life with more grace and even more joy. When we can be the best version of ourselves by incorporating more gratitude, everyone benefits. The entire planet and all species benefit from our engaging more with gratitude. How so, you may ask? How does a parrot in the Amazon or a koala in Australia benefit from humans being more grateful? The short answer is that everyone can benefit from the ripple-effect gratitude can have on life. This is a perspective that requires us to shift how we think about our own lives.

Consider this: If you are a pebble and you are thrown into water, you impact everything around you through a ripple effect. We know this to be true. The ripples may diminish in strength and size, but they still cause an effect. A ripple from a pebble will eventually reach a shore or bank. It may seem like nothing to a human, but an ant walking along a bit of dirt or sand might disagree when that tiny ripple raises the water level just enough to disturb the scent trail he's following or to provide him with an easy drink on a hot day.

The simple truth is that there are no benign or neutral ripples. Every ripple has an effect and touches something, even if you don't see it yourself.

Now think about the pebble. If you are a clean pebble, you make ripples in the water without changing the constitution of the water itself. However, if you are a dirty pebble, when you hit the water some of the dirt is going to sluff off and be carried out into the ripples.

Though both scenarios cause ripples which have an effect, the dirty pebble is having a different effect because it has changed the water slightly. If you are the dirty pebble, the ripples you create often include some bit of the dirt you carry. We don't always think of that, but it's true. Again, perhaps this may be imperceptible to some, but it is nonetheless true that every ripple impacts its environment in some way.

This simple truth then applies to humans: *We* impact our environment in some way, every day. By incorporating gratitude into our daily presence, we get to minimize the amount of dirt we bring into the water. As a result, we can diminish the negative impact our ripples have with the things we naturally create as humans. Gratitude creates cleaner versions of who we are, which is the person we bring into our environments.

Ultimately, this means that everyone and everything can benefit from gratitude. The water and everything our ripples touch can only benefit from our more balanced presence. As much as gratitude benefits us, personally, it also benefits everything around us. This, in turn, benefits us again, creating a cycle of positive reinforcement.

Though it may take time (and mass) for those ripples to have an effect on the parrot in the Amazon, the certainty is that they will, eventually. As long as we continue to focus on gratitude and move from our heads to our hearts, the choices we make will ultimately have a positive effect on the world around us. When we do so collectively, we can truly change the world for the better, benefitting everyone.

When Do We Need To Practice Gratitude?

"So it is not happiness that makes us grateful. It's grate-fulness that makes us happy."

– David Steindl-Rast

Practicing gratitude can happen at any time. It can be everything from a daily, hourly, or weekly practice to something that you incorporate as part of your life and being as you move from moment to moment.

There is no one way to engage with gratitude; the benefit remains whether it's routine by design or more spontaneous. What is true is that the benefit increases the more you engage with gratitude. So, one possible answer to the question, "When do we need to practice gratitude?" could simply be: Every time you think of it!

There are many helping professionals (therapists, coaches, teachers, gurus, etc.) who teach that gratitude needs to be a daily practice to realize its benefits. While you can realize benefits without a gratitude routine, creating a daily practice most often turns something into a habit, and habits are easier to expand on and maintain over time. There is a history of using gratitude journals for this, which is great. In fact, there are a lot of people in the world today who practice gratitude on a daily basis through keeping a gratitude journal and there are a lot of options when it comes to journaling in this way.[8] Ultimately, whatever works for you to connect with gratitude is a wonderful place to start.

The frequency (time, not vibration) with which you choose to engage in any practice is up to you. Ultimately, though, the routine you can maintain is the one you should be doing. If you can't maintain it, then it isn't working for you and it's time to try something else.

---

[8] See Resources for a QR code to download the *Daily Dose of Gratitude* page you can use to get started.

While keeping a gratitude journal can be really helpful, it's important to note that there is a difference between *identifying* gratitude and *feeling* gratitude. Keeping a journal and writing down what you are thankful for is not the same as deliberately pausing to *feel* what you are thankful for. In other words, there is a significant difference between stating what you are grateful for and actually *being* grateful.

So, if you keep a gratitude journal, the next step is to actually invite yourself to feel grateful after each item you enter. For example, if you write "I am grateful for a warm bed" in your journal, lift your pen, close your eyes, take a breath, and say, "thank you for this warm bed." Allow yourself to *feel* gratitude. Writing things you are grateful for keeps gratitude in a more theoretical place (still partially in your head), whereas expressing it places it fully in your heart. To further this experience, try this exercise:

- The next time you have your favorite morning beverage in your hands (we will use tea in this example), think to yourself "I am grateful for tea," then take a sip.

- Pause.

- Now, still holding the mug, look at the tea in your hands and think about it for a moment. While still looking at the tea, say aloud, "Thank you for this tea," and take a sip.

Did you feel the difference? Did you notice a deeper sense of presence in the second part? The difference between the two can be subtle, but powerful. In the first part, we are keeping gratitude outside of us by identifying it, but not truly feeling it. Whereas in the second part, we are inviting and allowing ourselves to *be* grateful.

Of course, the aspect of this exercise that most people struggle with is the lack of a specific person to thank in the second part. But, the truth is, you don't need someone to thank to express this type of internal gratitude. As you do the exercise, the sense of gratitude will flood your heart regardless. The key is to understand that being grateful feels different than identifying things to be grateful for. When you do the exercise—

when you experience the difference between stating gratitude and feeling gratitude—you slow down. If you slow down enough, you will feel it in your heart. While keeping a gratitude journal is a good place to start, ultimately, the practice that will transform your life more completely and create stronger, more positive ripples is *feeling* grateful.

The Good News!

The good news is that feeling grateful is something you can do anytime, anywhere, for anything. There is no routine or task attached to it, because it's more than that. It becomes part of your life in a way that doesn't need you to create a habit or use a checklist. Eventually, being grateful is something you inherently just are.

To get to that point, of course, you need to start somewhere. You need to engage in gratitude on a consistent basis in whatever way, with whatever timing, works for you. As long as it's authentic, and you invite yourself to feel grateful whenever you are identifying something to be grateful for, you will get there.

This also means that the answer to "When do we need to practice gratitude?" will one day become: All day, every day, because it's who I am.

Where Can We Practice Gratitude?

"There are so many things in the world that could be invisible to the material eye, and when you take a moment to stop, to pause, to be present and notice them—that's gratitude."

– Jay Shetty

The best part about gratitude is that it can be practiced anywhere, anytime, for anything! Gratitude is always available to you. Always, always, always. It is never not available. The beautiful thing is that you need nothing to allow yourself to access it. If you've grown accustomed to keeping a gratitude journal, it might feel as though you need the tools associated with journal-keeping in order to practice gratitude, but nothing could be further from the truth.

Ultimately, practicing gratitude incorporates anything that can help you live more in balance between your head and your heart. While it can include stating what you're grateful for, it's about allowing yourself to feel grateful, and feelings require nothing but your presence.

This means that you can engage with gratitude anywhere, on any day, in any hour, or for any minute of your life. Sitting in a meeting at work? You can think for a second and remember that morning's coffee and feel grateful. Stuck in traffic? You can go into your mind and think of a song you love and feel grateful. Trying to organize your garage? You can look around you, see anything that gives you a smile, and feel grateful. The possibilities are endless.

Gratitude is not limited to the "big ticket" items in our life. Nor is it limited to the confines of a pen and paper or a keyboard. Gratitude is available to us every second of our lives for any reason. It's a choice we get to make. This is the best part about gratitude.

If you don't think it is available to you, stop what you are doing right now and look out a window or at something in your environment. Look at something that makes your heart smile and you will be in a state of gratitude.

You don't even need to say the words "I'm grateful for..." or "thank you."

You can feel gratitude just by looking at something or remembering something and dropping into your heart.

It is impossible to not be in a state of gratitude when you look at your life and find something that makes you smile. That is the beauty of gratitude: It is always available and it can be done anywhere at any time for any reason about anything. When you understand this, you can take it a step further, because you realize that living from a state of gratitude is a form of superpower.

Gratitude Is a Superpower

Practicing gratitude is amazing, because it's like having the ability to hot-wire your brain, your body, your soul, your heart, and your mind all at once. Every aspect of you is enhanced and improved by practicing gratitude. This is why a gratitude practice is often part of wellness programs; it's like having a secret key to unlock all the feel-good endorphins that we need (and that a lot of people chase). How lucky are you to know that you don't have to "chase" anything? You just have to pause and invite yourself into a state of gratitude.

When you allow yourself to live from a grateful place, you create a healthier relationship with yourself, which can lead to healthier and happier relationships with others. It really is that powerful.

So, where can you practice gratitude? Anywhere and everywhere... and you should! Do it right now. Just look around you and find one thing, just one thing that makes your heart smile, and feel grateful for it. You'll be glad you did.

Why Is Gratitude Important?

"Human beings, by changing the inner attitudes of their minds, can change the outer aspects of their lives."

– William James

Gratitude changes your life completely. It is the one life hack that can instantly change everything, from how you're feeling to what you're thinking. Furthermore, over time, it shifts your perspective as well as your energy. The frequencies running through your body move in response to gratitude, for the better. This means that gratitude is important because we need gratitude both as a tool and as a way of being.

Life can be hard, but gratitude can help make it easier.

Engaging with gratitude is also important because it does not require a lot of time or any special knowledge, effort, or understanding. Everybody knows what it means to feel thankful or express gratitude, even children and animals.

This makes it different from some of the other tools, perspectives, or studies that can change your life completely, like manifesting (which is great, but requires proper study to truly be effective).

Feeling gratitude is something you can do that will instantly change you. It changes your thinking, your feelings, your cells, even your face. When you are grateful, your face softens and you smile more because you actually have happier chemicals running through your body. You show up differently, which can cause people around you to show up differently, too.

This is an important aspect of gratitude that isn't as frequently discussed.

When you practice gratitude, your world can change, and you need to allow it to happen. For example, people who are generally unkind may tend to fall away from your life more because they struggle to be around somebody who is in a happier place. They haven't figured out how to be with someone who prioritizes their own well-being and it becomes uncomfortable for them, so they tend to go away. As much as it can hurt sometimes, you have to let them leave. They have their own journey to take.

Perhaps your example can serve to be an inspiration for them. Perhaps you changing your life for the better will give them permission to do the same. Or perhaps they're just not ready or in a place to want to change anything. All of this is okay.

Being in gratitude is always an internal job, because nobody can do it for you or force you to feel gratitude. Sometimes when a practice of gratitude is thrust upon you (such as during a dinner in which everyone is expected to cite something they are grateful for) it can feel false or inauthentic. It's okay to decline the practice in those instances, just as it's okay to participate. What matters is that you know that gratitude is personal and that your practice will always be (and ought to be) unique to you.

What's most important is that you figure out how you can best engage with gratitude in a way that brings you to a place of actually embodying gratitude in your life—living each day with gratitude as if it were part of the blood in your veins or the breath in your lungs. That's how important gratitude can be, and is.

But I Don't Feel Grateful...

"By writing what I was grateful for, I learned to look for things that made me smile."

– Dr. Ranjani Rao

Though life can at times feel overwhelming, gratitude is always an option. Bad days and bad things will almost always happen. We can never fully escape them. On those days, or in those circumstances, the key is to realize that you do not have to feel grateful for everything all the time and you can use gratitude to help shift your mood or emotions, even momentarily. This can give you more mental and emotional real estate when you need it most.

How Can You Create Gratitude When Things Are Bad?

When embodying gratitude is a challenge, you can make the decision to just focus on one thing at a time. Instead of abandoning the practice completely, focus on something little that brings you joy or makes you feel grateful.

There is a simple trick to support you when things are bad: You can create a prompt to remind you that gratitude exists as a tool—especially when access to the feeling of gratitude is difficult. There are many different things you can prompt yourself to do, including:

- Listening to a meditation
- Reading a book or journal
- Attending a class, such as art or yoga
- Calling a friend or loved one

The goal is to engage in something that slows you down long enough to shift your focus and presence, which makes the possibilities almost endless. You can look around you and find something that makes you feel good. You can set a reminder in your phone, for example, to go off at the same time every day prompting you to pause and look at your environment and find something that makes your heart smile.

When life is bad or when things are a struggle, if you can remind yourself to find something to engage with and feel grateful for, it will help.

A Note About Gratitude and Guilt

Sometimes, when the world around us feels heavy or like it's falling apart, and we look at our own lives and see that they are generally good in comparison, we can feel guilty. This is normal and not something to shame yourself about or prevent you from engaging in gratitude. In fact, it's probably even more important for you to acknowledge your blessings with gratitude in these moments. Think back to the pebble and the ripples and know that feeling guilt or shame about your situation doesn't help anyone; it just muddies the waters. Instead, allow yourself to feel grateful and then, if you're so inclined, find a way to help others. In other words, spread the blessings, the gratitude, and the love.

Gratitude is meant to be easy, so don't make it too hard. Keeping it simple will help you have more success. When I say to find something in your environment, it can be the simplicity of feeling grateful for a warm blanket on a cold day or ice in your water on a hot one. It can be as simple as somebody smiling at you at the checkout line in a store or seeing a dog walk down the street. It can even be as simple as enjoying a piece of chocolate or hearing a bird singing in the morning or just feeling the sun on your face.

To truly be in gratitude, you do not have to be grateful for winning the lottery or something else that is massive, heroic, or extraordinary. In fact, it's gratitude that helps us see the everyday, ordinary things as extraordinary. That is why when life is hard, engaging with gratitude can help make it a little easier.

Even on the smallest scale for the most mundane things that you can think of—like warm socks on a cold day—gratitude is what changes things for the better. You just have to remember to take a moment to access it.

How Do We Create A Life Of Gratitude?

"The number one joy indicator, the one thing that will predict whether someone feels joy in their life or not, is the practice of gratitude."

– John O'Leary

A life of gratitude is created by choosing a place to start and then making a commitment to a practice. As we've already explored, this practice can be daily or not. It can even be multiple times a day. What matters is that it's something you can be consistent with, while also leaving room for flexibility and growth. In this way, you will create the most optimal situation for turning a practice into something you embody—something you become.

This means that if you do it enough to make it a reflexive behavior, it will be something that changes your presence; one day you will realize that you just show up that way.

That's the important thing to note: A life of gratitude—an attitude of gratitude, as it's sometimes referred to—does not happen overnight. It requires commitment and a desire to change. Once you start down the path, as you begin to realize positive results from your efforts (such as feeling more inner peace or more joy), the process becomes self-reinforcing. It starts to feel like you can't imagine *not* living from a place of gratitude.

Once that has become your reality, you will know that you have truly created a life of gratitude, one in which you will always be able to find balance, calm, and joy. Though each path needs to be uniquely designed, here is a suggestion on how you can create a practice that goes from task to embodiment in three months:

Four Steps to Embodying Gratitude

STEP 1: Start with a gratitude journal – Begin by writing down three things each night that you are grateful for and why. Be specific; for example, don't write "friends" but write down a specific friend and what they did or why you are grateful for them. I like using the formula of "Person–Place–Thing" for this exercise. Do this for 3–4 weeks.

STEP 2: Add mornings to your practice – Start your day with gratitude. When you wake, carve out 15 minutes to revisit your list from the night before. When you do, sit with each item for a minute, allowing yourself to **feel** grateful again. Once you've done this, think of your day ahead and write down three things you are grateful for. Do this for 3–4 weeks while still doing the evening practice.

STEP 3: Practice saying "thank you" – After 6–8 weeks of journaling both morning and night, add a new practice to your day, by specifically saying thank you for something specific. Since we all need to drink something everyday, that can be something easy to focus on for this exercise, so we will use it as an example.

Sometime during your day when you are drinking something, pause, look at your beverage, and take a moment. After reflecting for a bit, say thank you. You do not have to say thank you to anyone or anything in particular; you are simply being in a state of gratitude for the beverage. You could be thanking the farmer for the tea leaves, the cow for the milk, or yourself for hydrating with water. It doesn't matter. What matters is that you are deliberately putting yourself into a state of gratitude. Do this for another 3–4 weeks, while still journaling in the morning and evening.

STEP 4: Take stock and reflect – Look back on the 9–12 weeks of changes you have made and reflect on what pieces made you feel more gratitude. Ask yourself what you would change. What would you do more of, or less of? What else can you focus on? Adjust accordingly, and keep going!

Ultimately, gratitude starts as a choice. You have to choose to focus on gratitude before it can become a reflex. Furthermore, you have to choose it consistently over a period of time for it to become part of your being.

Most importantly, it's a choice only you can make (nobody can make it for you), but it's a choice that will be worth the effort.

What Is Possible With More Gratitude?

"Behind every creative act is a statement of love. Every artistic creation is a statement of gratitude."

– Kilroy J. Oldster

It is true that adopting gratitude as a way of being benefits you and can positively impact your world, but what else can it do?

The short answer is: A lot.

Understanding gratitude and applying it in your life leads to more empathy, more connection, more compassion, and more empowerment, to name just a few of its benefits. These, in turn, lead to a stronger and better quality of life, which leads to healthier decisions, which leads to more investment in yourself and others, which leads to a better community, which can lead to better and healthier societies. And so on and so forth.

This, of course, doesn't happen overnight, but can happen in only a couple generations, if we allow it. The possibilities that gratitude can create are almost endless.

Why Does Gratitude Create Infinite Possibility?

As we said at the very beginning: *Gratitude takes you from your head to your heart.*

Of course, the mind is a home for the entire range of emotions, from fear to love. It processes everything we are feeling and gives it meaning and significance, or not. The head is where we try to sort out our thoughts and feelings simultaneously, some-times resulting in more confusion. When we say our "head was spinning" this is what we mean.

When we are trying to make sense of something that we can't properly organize, mentally, emotionally, or intellectually, the mind will work overtime. To try and accomplish this, we can cycle through more thoughts and more emotions as it churns, which can often feel chaotic. While the head processes all of our emotions, it is specifically the home for the low-frequency emotions, such as: fear, anger, frustration, hate, insecurity, annoyance, isolation, etc. Conversely, these emotions rarely (if ever) reside in our hearts. Though the high-frequency emotions (love, joy, peace) can be present in the head, especially as you are trying to figure something out, they predominantly live in our hearts.

The main difference between the head and the heart, therefore, is that the heart is the home for high-frequency emotions, and these are the emotions that invite us to create a better world for ourselves and others. When we are in our hearts, we make different decisions and ask different questions. We want to know how things will benefit others, not how we can avoid something. We ask proactive questions, rather than making reactive statements.

Living from the heart is what creates more connection and better solutions, such as:

- It allows us to recognize that we are a part of something, not apart from something.

- It allows us to take perspective (which is a superpower, as we have already discussed in the segment on compassion) and build or create new, healthier ways of being.

In short, the heart is the realm of innovation, creativity, and of asking: *What's possible?* To get back to the heart when we are stuck in our head or when things have gone awry, we can use gratitude.

Living From a Place of Gratitude

When we practice gratitude, we ultimately move to *living* from a place of gratitude. When that happens, we are shifting to living from a heart-centered place—one where anything becomes possible because we are accessing the higher-frequency emotions on a regular basis while decreasing the presence of low-frequency emotions.

So, what is possible with more gratitude? The answer is simple: Everything. **Everything becomes possible with more gratitude, both personally and globally.**

There's a reason videos of animals in the wild expressing gratitude go viral, such as when a dolphin brings "presents" to someone that helped its mate get out of a fishing net or when a crow brings shiny gifts to a human that has fed it.

We see it and we recognize it for what it is… and it makes us feel good.

We feel happy because we know that someone made life better for someone else, and it was acknowledged with gratitude as a kindness received.

This creates a sense of goodness, which somewhat ties back to the philosophers that linked gratitude to justice. We know goodness and acts of kindness when we see them, and we like to reward them.

We reward them by expressing gratitude.

When we set up this cyclical system of goodness and gratitude, we are essentially building a kinder, more connected society. In other words, gratitude helps to make better things possible… and maybe, even probable.

Conclusion

"If the only prayer you said in your whole life was, 'thank you,' that would suffice."

– Meister Eckhart

By now, hopefully you realize the power of gratitude and its incredible potential in your life. Understanding gratitude is, in some ways, about understanding how to create and live a better life, both individually and collectively.

We know that gratitude gives us instant access to higher-frequency emotions by moving us from our heads to our hearts. We also know that, to be most effective, gratitude can (and should) evolve from a habit or practice to an embodiment.

We need to adopt gratitude as a way of being in our lives in order to realize it fully. We do this by building a relationship with gratitude everyday through creating a habit. By identifying the things for which we are grateful, we can then learn how to express those feelings on a regular basis. We know that this will transform our lives for the better, sometimes resulting in changes in our relationships, which is okay. Ultimately, by embodying gratitude, we know that we can have a positive impact that has the potential to be far-reaching.

This is the good news of gratitude: The fact that something as simple as feeling grateful for the small everyday things in our lives can ultimately transform our world for the better. In that regard, gratitude, it seems, is more than a feeling or a tool, it's a way forward. It's a roadmap to a better world with more kindness and greater connection… one cup of tea or pair of socks, at a time!

UNDERSTANDING

KARMA

"Every action of our lives touches on some chord
that will vibrate in eternity."

Edwin Hubbell Chapin

Introduction

"Our lives are not our own. We are bound to others, past and present, and by each crime and every kindness, we birth our future."

– David Mitchell

Karma is a word many people use without truly understanding the depth of its significance. As such, it is often invoked when someone has felt wronged or wishes to place blame on others— to invoke penalty with detachment from a place of judgment. Most notably, Karma is usually referred to in a singular, externalized direction, as in: "Karma's only a bitch if you are." This means that most people don't consider themselves to be a bitch, but may find it easy to identify others this way.

As one of the Universal Laws, however, Karma is devoid of these human-based judgments and subjectivity. Like energy, Karma simply is. In these pages, you will learn some of the basics about Karma… the proverbial Who, What, When, Where, Why, and How. More importantly, you will also discover tools you can use to help you heal your Karma, leading to forgiveness and freedom—the ultimate goal.

If you've ever been curious about how Karma really works, or if you have wanted to have a better understanding of Karma and how you can apply this understanding in your own life, then you're in the right place and this is for you. Now, let's start with the most basic question: Why is this important?

Why It's Important to Understand Karma

On our journey through life (or through lifetimes), we accumulate Karma—both good and less-good. This is part of being human. "Earth School" (as it is sometimes referred to) is about learning. We (our souls) are here to engage with life in a way that supports our evolution and growth, so that the collective can also grow and so that we can eventually return to oneness.

Life, however, can get messy in (very) human ways. Sometimes we behave kindly and sometimes we don't. Sometimes we receive things that hurt just as we sometimes hurt others; and sometimes we receive things that heal or we help others to heal. Throughout our life, we are both the recipient and the perpetrator.

By understanding Karma and how we can engage with it on a regular basis, we get to have an impact on how often the good outweighs the less-good. We get to choose how we show up for ourselves and others, which is the best gift we can both give and receive. Karma simply is, which means we cannot escape it, nor should we want to. This is why it's important to truly understand Karma, instead of seeing it as some external force and arbitrary tool for passing judgment on others.

Instead, we should do our best to understand it so that we can work with it and create a better life for ourselves and others. At the end of the day, that's what I have found that most people ultimately desire. Working with your Karma can help make that happen.

What Is Karma?

"Your believing or not believing in karma has no effect on its existence, nor on its consequences to you. Just as a refusal to believe in the ocean would not prevent you from drowning."

– F. Paul Wilson

Karma is one of the Universal Laws, as we understand them. In my opinion, it is most similar to the Law of Energy, which states simply that "everything is energy," as we've already discussed. Karma, like energy, is both tangible and intangible. We can know it and experience it, and we can impact it, but we can't always understand or quantify it. It just is—which is what makes it a Universal Law.

What is a Universal Law?

A Universal Law is a principle that exists at the core of the universe, which means that it applies "universally" regardless of any other factors, including time, place, and situation. These "laws" are more like rules or conditions that explain (and possibly determine) how the universe works and is designed. They are immutable, meaning they can't be changed, because they simply are.

Even though Karma seems to be universally understood and applied across multiple religions, practices, and beliefs, it can also be looked at through other lenses. We can explore Karma through the physicality of life (and lifetimes) as well as the more intangible aspect of thought.

All of these approaches serve to provide parameters and understanding for Karma's application, but they don't alter the underlying rule which is ultimately about action. As such, we always need to return to the most basic approach to understanding Karma, which is very succinctly stated in The Golden Rule: *Do unto others as you would have them do unto you.* "Do" is the operative word here, because Karma is about action.

Karma and The Golden Rule

Some variation of The Golden Rule can be found in virtually every belief system on the planet practiced by humans. For many, it provides a moral compass that has its basis in an ethical understanding that we are all connected and part of something greater, whether that's community, society, the species, or the planet as a whole—or all of the above. The rule is set forth as a guiding principle of behavior that invites the individual to consider the consequences of their actions before they are undertaken. The key words in that statement are: behavior and consequences.

The Golden Rule, just like Karma, is ultimately about action. Our deeds have an impact on everything around us, just as everything happening around us can have an impact on our decisions about what to do next. Everything is connected.

Therefore, possibly the best way to understand Karma and how it works is to think of a boomerang: Whatever you put out will come back to you... eventually. When it comes to Karma, the most important word in that sentence is "eventually." Understanding that Karma is universal means that time does not apply, at least not in the way we understand it as humans. Karma is part of the collective whole of the universe, which means that sometimes the scales are balanced quite immediately and sometimes they can take lifetimes. But they will always balance.

In short, what you give is what you will receive. Always. Eventually.

When Does Karma Happen?

"Everything that is in the heavens, on earth, and under the earth is penetrated with connectedness, penetrated with relatedness."

– Hildegard von Bingen

When we think about Karma, it helps to incorporate a basic understanding of lifetimes. Since Karma is universal, it doesn't use human time in its application. Depending on your belief system, this may (or may not) be something you can align with. But, even if you only believe in having one lifetime as a human, Karma still applies—perhaps even more so, as you would seemingly want to both balance and move the scales upward during a very short and specific timeframe.

For the practices that teach a birth-rebirth cycle, it might be a little bit easier to grasp, as there is a longer trajectory through which we can apply the principles of Karma. Either way, Karma applies regardless of your beliefs. To follow are just two examples of how different beliefs incorporate Karma in their practice:

- In Hinduism, there are different words for Karma based on lifetimes. Specifically for "this lifetime" the word is: Prarabdha. This refers to the Karma that is sown and reaped during this specific time of being alive. The word that refers to Karma that is carried forward from a past life is: Samchita. And finally, the word for Karma that awaits the soul in a future lifetime is: Kriyamana.

- Conversely, Buddhism considers Karma to be part of the cycle of birth and rebirth, with no specific delineation between lifetimes. Therefore, the soul is free from all Karma when it no longer needs to reincarnate.

These two variations are often the most traditionally understood ideas when it comes to Karma. They are also usually blended into one simple principle that is best expressed by the old adage: *You reap what you sow.*

This is true, regardless of which lifetime you are in. Unfortunately, the concept of multiple lifetimes can be seen as both overwhelming and (potentially) a cop-out where Karma is concerned. If our actions have no identifiable consequences in this lifetime because they can be carried over, what's the point of managing our Karma account now? The short answer is: Because it's the best option... for everyone. So, why wouldn't you?

If the Universal Law of Karma is to be understood and accepted, then another old adage is also relevant: There's no time like the present!

Without being privy to the Divine Blueprint of the universe and its ultimate wisdom in timing, the best option is to do our best now, and always. That way, we know we are helping ourselves to be free of karmic patterns in the future, as well as helping make the world a better place for everyone along the way.

Altruistic? Yes. But no less true, powerful, or important.

It's from this more general perspective that we will focus on understanding Karma.

Who Can You Have Karma With?

"How people treat you is their Karma; how you react is yours."

– Wayne Dyer, PhD

The short answer to who you can have Karma with is: Anyone, but not necessarily everyone, in your life. In truth, it's a bit more probable that you have Karma with people who are consistently in your life so that you can work on the Karma together. These often include:

- **Soul Family** – Most often these are people who are your actual family and friends.
- **Soul Pod** – Typically, these are "adjacent" people in your life, like coworkers.
- **Soul Mirrors** – These are people whose Divine Plan aligns or intersects with yours.

For the most part, you can look at karmic contracts and all of these relationship groups through the lens of: Reason/Season/Lifetime. Each individual in the above groups will fall into one of these categories.

Furthermore, people within these groups can move between categories, especially once the Karma is completed. For example, a lifetime person can become seasonal, just as a reason person can become lifetime. A lot depends on the karmic contract and how/if you (and they) have chosen to show up to complete it.

Lifetime/Reason/Season Karmic Relationships

Lifetime Karmic Relationships are the most common, which means that these are the relationships we have with people who are consistently in our life. It also means that the karmic healing and lessons can come and go in waves. Like a spiral, we move through these patterns with this person, continually leveling up in between periods of neutrality, calm, and peace. These relationships allow us the most grace as we heal from Karma, as these are often the people who stay with us, regardless of what's happening.

Reason Karmic Relationships are the ones that serve a single purpose to help us learn or remember something we needed to overcome. You will know it was a Reason-based Karmic Relationship when the person is simply no longer part of your life. Once the lesson was learned, the Karma was allowed to resolve. Unfortunately, many people fall into the trap of trying to make the person stay (which creates new Karma), rather than seeing it for the gift it is and letting it end.

Season Karmic Relationships serve to create opportunities for growth during a specific period of your life. Once the period is done, the relationship usually ends or the person can move into one of the other categories.

~~~~~

Another aspect of karmic relationships is that you can have Karma with all of these individuals at the same time. It is often assumed that a karmic relationship has to have strife and cause chaos or struggle in your life. While this can be true, it's not always the case. Some karmic relationships move smoothly through reconciliation with you barely noticing.

A good example might be if you had a coworker who was a close friend for the years in which you worked together, but once you changed jobs, you barely saw each other. You probably taught each other a lot during the time you were together, helping each other to grow and learn, while resolving issues between you. But because it was coupled with a work setting with specific or more obvious parameters and boundaries, you may not have noticed any sort of direct struggle.

Regardless of whether you are aware of a karmic relationship or not, ultimately the goal will always be your own personal soul growth. This is why it is important to understand how Karma shows up in your life, especially in relationships.

Where Can You Work On Your Karma?

"The meaning of karma is in the intention. The intention behind action is what matters."

– The Bhagavad Gita

Karmic healing is always available to you. Karma can be worked on anywhere at any time. It is not limited to a specific place, time, or environment. In fact, healing Karma is most effective when it becomes part of your everyday life.

When you view Karma as a way of being, rather than a task to be achieved or crossed off a list, you will experience greater freedom and peace more easily and more readily. Healing Karma is about aligning your behaviors through shifting your mindset.

Interestingly, I have sometimes heard people link having a karmic mindset to being selfish—doing good in order to receive good. Nothing could be further from the truth. However, if being "selfish" in this way is what first brings you to the table, that is still a place to start, and starting is what matters. Once you have begun shifting your perspective on Karma, you may notice feeling more balanced as you experience a greater connection to your own being and to the world around you. This will lead to feelings of empowerment and peace, ultimately resulting in the freedom and joy so many seek.

As with everything, there are best practices for understanding and healing your Karma. These can include both solo and group activities, such as meditation, volunteering, journaling, and more! Again, what matters is that you get started with a clear intention and understanding.

Examples of Solo Activities

Individual endeavors to heal Karma often involve activities that are both introspective and reflective. This can include: therapy/counseling, journaling, meditation, and movement, such as yoga or tai chi.

What all of these activities have in common is the opportunity they create for deeper connection to self. Knowing yourself better is what allows you to show up in life better. This then provides more opportunity to heal your Karma. Yes, it really can be that simple.

Examples of Group Activities

Participating in groups can be a beneficial method of healing Karma, because they provide a safe space to explore our connections, feelings, and thoughts. They also allow for feedback and support, unlike solo activities. Some group activities can be deliberately focused on creating healing, such as retreats, support groups, or counseling. Whereas other activities, like volunteering, can create an environment for connection and understanding, which can also lead to healing.

Both solo and group endeavors are ultimately about action. To start healing and using a karmic mindset, you have to show up and you have to *do* something. You can't heal your Karma solely by sitting in meditation all day or just journaling. You have to get involved with life in order to use the momentum of life to support you in your process. Just like most Karma shows up in relationships of some kind, you can't create growth by isolating or living in a bubble.

If you are willing to be present and involved, you will create opportunities to heal your Karma and improve your life.

Why Do We Have Karma?

"Karma, when properly understood, is just the mechanics through which consciousness manifests."

– Deepak Chopra

What is the purpose of Karma? This is a question I have been asked many times throughout my career. While physical evolution is highly tangible and visible, karmic evolution is somewhat more subjective… unless you look at it with a much wider perspective. And though there may be nuances to the answer based on the person asking, there is a single statement that applies to everyone: Karma is a tool that helps us evolve as a species, on an emotional and spiritual level.

We may need to apply it individually at first, but ultimately, collective growth will eventually come into play. For example, the industrial revolution prompted many countries to adopt laws that prevent the exploitation of children as workers. This could be viewed as a karmic evolution for the species. But where did it begin? Most likely, it began with individuals. All it takes is for one person to begin questioning the way things are—and to see a way that could be better—for different decisions to be made.

Understanding that our actions are not isolated events and that they can create ripple effects throughout our communities and world is a first step in understanding how important it is to be mindful of one's own Karma. Karma is about action, not just thought, as it's the different actions that create different results, thereby impacting one's Karma, and eventually the Karma of an entire society.

It all starts with us, though, so let's take a look at how our personal Karma plays a role.

Individually, our souls are on their own journey toward oneness. What does this mean? It means that we have come to "Earth School" to learn, remember, and apply those lessons in ways that fuel our spiritual evolution. Whether you understand that it's for one lifetime or many lifetimes, the goal remains the same.

In order to achieve this, we need opportunities to show ourselves what we have remembered as well as opportunities to learn new things. In most cases, these both come as life lessons, such as: patience, tolerance, kindness, and love. The greatest tool we can use to learn these lessons, therefore resides in the ability to take perspective.[9] By seeing ourselves in another's shoes, we create an opportunity to understand and make better decisions—for ourselves and for the whole. Ultimately, this elevates everyone and everything as we create a better world, together, and it all starts with our individual Karma.

---

[9] If you skipped forward, the Understanding Compassion segment explains the power of taking perspective in greater detail.

How Do You Heal Karma?

"The wound is the place where the light enters you."

– Rumi

Though many people may believe that they need to go to a shaman or other esoteric practitioner to help them heal their Karma, this is not true. Healing Karma is predominantly an inside job, meaning it has to start from within you. Of course, good practitioners can provide guidance, but that is all. To heal your Karma, you need four specific things: Willingness, Guidance, Deliberate Attention, and Consistency.

Willingness – When a person is ready—truly ready—to begin working on their Karma, willingness is the first step. A commitment to show up, take perspective, and create change is the only way to begin. This step requires some measure of humility, too, as we must admit that we have most likely treated others as we have been treated... somewhere along the way. This can often be a hard truth to swallow for many.

In fact, one of the greatest hurdles in healing Karma is a person's desire to hold on to the belief that it is a one-way street. Many people find it difficult to accept that they may have wronged others as they feel wronged, but it's always the first step in healing and understanding how Karma actually works. When you are committed to healing your Karma, you know the rebalancing is always in progress, and you accept that you have behaved as both the giver and receiver.

Guidance – As previously mentioned, you can find assistance in healing Karma from external sources, such as esoteric practitioners. This can be a positive form of support and is often a requirement since many people don't know where to begin.

Guidance from a helping professional can come in many forms, such as: teaching tools, sharing learned wisdom, and providing emotional support. Ultimately, however, it is important to remember that a practitioner cannot do the work for you.

Deliberate Attention – In order to heal your Karma, you must first raise your awareness to your existing habits and behaviors so that you can pay deliberate attention to changing them. While it would be easy to call this step "awareness" or just "attention," it's more than that. The addition of the word "deliberate" implies a conscious approach to taking action. In other words, your intention matters. By making your attention deliberate, you are also making it focused. Focused attention generates better results.

Consistency – Once you have identified what it is that you need to change, the key to healing is to remain consistent. This is a process; it's not a one-and-done endeavor. Being consistent in your commitment will lead to healing. This is what it means to create a new mindset. When you do, your actions come from a different place. Consistency leads to the shift in mindset, which ultimately leads to a shift in your presence. This is what heals your Karma.

What If I Already Wished Harm?

"The best way to find yourself is to lose yourself in the service of others."

– Mahatma Gandhi

Of course, there are times in our life when we wish we could take things back that we may have said or done. There are also times when we start to realize we weren't behaving at our best in the past. This usually happens when we raise our awareness and shift our perspective. While we can't change our karmic past, we *can* influence its future. We can do this by changing the present and undoing any harm we may have caused... if we keep our awareness high.

To begin, it is possible to interrupt the creation of Karma if you have recently wished harm on another person. "Recently" and "interrupt" are the key words to remember in this situation. Due to their nature, they are intertwined with one another, but they are also somewhat subjective.

When it comes to Karma from a human perspective, "recent" can mean anytime from the last few seconds to within one day. The more recent the behavior, the greater the success in reversing it. "Interrupting" means stopping in transit. With regard to Karma, it means stopping in creation. There is a reason why Karma isn't immediate: It allows for humans to be fallible... and to change their mind. Thankfully.

Steps to Interrupt, Reverse, and Undo Harm

While there may be more ways to address this situation, here are two of the simplest ways to interrupt any harm you may have directly or inadvertently wished upon someone.

"Cancel and Purify"

Sometimes our emotions get the better of us and we say things we regret or don't really mean. Sometimes we mean them but think better of it later. If it's only been a few minutes, you can interrupt this event by saying "Cancel and Purify" aloud or in your head.

This is something I learned a long time ago from a trusted friend. It's a way of telling the universe that you didn't mean what you just thought or said. This phrase asks for help in neutralizing the thought or statement, thereby shifting the energy behind it to one that no longer does harm. Of course, you have to mean it when you say it or it won't work, but it's one of the simplest and fastest ways to begin to hold yourself accountable and shift your presence.

Lifting Others Up

If it has been a little longer than a few minutes, you can take a different approach and make amends. Amends can look like actually atoning and asking for forgiveness, or it can look like changing your actions and engaging in a life-enhancing behavior, or both!

What is a life-enhancing behavior? It can be anything from volunteering and offering kindness, to making anonymous donations or anything else that is focused on lifting others up.

Beautifully, this action can also look like offering a blessing. Blessings are universal and always aligned with a recipient's highest good. This means that, unlike prayer, you are not attaching to the outcome or imposing your will; you are simply offering the best to someone.

Whichever approach you take, it takes courage to remember that it's not good to wish harm on others, even if you are experiencing pain yourself, perhaps especially then. Choosing to interrupt and undo the harm you may have caused is a powerful way to realign your Karma to one that is more healing and connected to spiritual growth.

Why Heal Your Karma?

"You cannot do a kindness too soon, for you never know how soon it will be too late."

– Ralph Waldo Emerson

Healing anything in your life can lead to positive results. Most specifically, healing often leads to some measure of freedom. In the case of Karma, healing can also bring forth forgiveness. Both forgiveness and healing create freedom. When it comes to Karma, the good news is that you don't have to do it with the other person present. There are numerous ways to go about this and I've included some suggestions in the coming pages.

But first, we need to look at why you should want to heal your Karma. To do that, we need to take a deeper look at healing, forgiveness, and freedom and the roles they play in our lives. Here is brief summary of each:

- **Healing is self-focused.** It's a process by which we connect more deliberately with ourselves in meaningful ways, resulting in a greater sense of well-being and (potentially) opening the door to forgiveness.

- **Forgiveness is other-focused.** It's a process that allows us to have a deeper understanding of our relationships as well as our behaviors and the behaviors of others. Engaging in forgiveness also results in greater connection to self, enhanced well-being, and freedom.

- **Freedom is life/soul-focused.** Freedom is the result of deep connection to self and soul, which is often the result of the work done by healing past wounds, fixing dysfunctional patterns of behavior, and understanding the relationship one has to something greater—either the Divine, or on a more human level, community or society. Freedom is the highest state of well-being one can achieve.

All three are aspects of healing Karma have their own process and attributes. Ultimately, it's up to you how you want to move through healing your Karma. The important thing is to start.

Healing Is Self-Focused

"When you plant a seed of love, it is you that blossoms."
– Ma Jaya Sati Bhagavati

Healing (including healing your Karma) is something you have to do yourself. However, you can enlist the help of others—especially professionals—to guide and support you on your healing journey. Ultimately, though, nobody can do the work *for* you; however, they can do it *with* you and alongside you.

Asking for professional help is a sign of strength, not weakness. Reaching out to an expert when you are in need takes courage. Too often, people worry about the opinion of others, rather than worrying about their own healing journey. Sadly, there is still stigma around seeking help for mental health issues, though we do see evidence of that changing. Thankfully. The important step is to start by asking.

To find the best helping professional for you and your situation, it is good to consult with people you trust in your life. If reaching out to a professional is not available to you, there are other resources you can find to help you as you work to heal your Karma, which often include looking inward and engaging in self-care practices.

The Inward Journey

Healing is self-focused because it requires an inward journey. Whether you are seeking emotional, spiritual, or physical karmic healing, you will need to create a deeper connection to yourself. To heal, you need to know yourself better and more clearly. This is especially true when you are focusing on spiritual or emotional Karma.

Though the inward journey can, at times, feel overwhelming, it's also true that the more you allow yourself to connect with and experience your feelings, thoughts, and emotions, the easier it will become. This is because the very nature of these things is that they are fluid, constantly in motion. By acknowledging your current thought, feeling, or emotion, you allow the next one in line to come forward, prompting the one you are experiencing to move on. Conversely, if you try to ignore or push away the emotion or thought, what you are doing is simply creating the equivalent of a closed-circuit loop. The thought or emotion will continue to eat up your emotional and mental real estate in the background until you can acknowledge it.

Part of the karmic healing journey is recognizing that these types of reactions (thoughts and emotions) are temporary and allowing them to be—acknowledging instead of acting on them. Bringing this level of awareness is part of the shift that happens when you place deliberate attention on your Karma. It's also a key component to not creating more Karma while allowing yourself to heal.

Forgiveness Is Other-Focused

"To forgive is to set a prisoner free and discover that the prisoner was you."

– Lewis B. Smedes

Forgiveness is most often about something external, which is why it's considered "other-focused." However, the effects of forgiveness are always internal. The external component is a requirement because we are talking about Karma, which often involves others. There is, of course, self-forgiveness, but that is more often related to other internal issues, which aren't often correlated to Karma, but rather are part of mental health.

As such, when discussing healing Karma, forgiveness is a tool that can be used to "unshackle" yourself from another person and the karmic contract you may have. This process is a great step onto the path of Karmic healing and involves three simple truths:

- **Forgiveness is not one-and-done.** Though forgiveness requires a single initial step, it often also needs ongoing awareness on your part to shift your perspective.

- **Forgiveness is always a choice.** Though it can feel hard to forgive someone, it is always an option and always a choice. It is never removed from you or controlled by someone else, because forgiveness comes from within you.

- **Forgiveness is not condoning or forgetting an event.** Forgiveness is about reclaiming your emotional power around an event, rather than letting it control you. It's also about helping you create boundaries, if necessary, especially for future events.

Choosing Forgiveness

When you make the choice to forgive, you are giving a gift to yourself and to your future! Forgiveness may require an external component (such as someone or something to forgive), but ultimately it is a solo act and a choice you get to make.

Since forgiveness is a choice, it's also never too late, especially if you would like to heal your Karma. Furthermore, it's never too soon. In fact, since it is a gift you give yourself, the sooner you can do it, the better.

Finally, it bears noting that you can forgive without having to tell the other person. You can forgive them and move on, with or without letting them know. So, if the idea of sharing forgiveness with someone is holding you back, know that it doesn't need to. You can still forgive.

Freedom Is Life- and Soul-Focused

"My actions are my only true belongings. I cannot escape the consequences of my actions. My actions are the ground upon which I stand."

– Thich Nhat Hanh

Freedom is about more than being free from oppression, fear, or any other low-frequency emotion or situation, though that is clearly an integral piece of the equation. Freedom is also about feeling empowered and having agency over your own life. The proverbial "pursuit of happiness" is most successful when it includes freedom. In fact, I would argue that it's only truly successful when it includes freedom.

When you work on healing your Karma and resolving your soul's lessons, you take steps toward the ultimate goal of freedom. This is why freedom is both life- and soul-focused. It enhances your life in the present moment, just as it helps your soul in its evolution. Healing your Karma, therefore, is an important step to creating more freedom in your head and heart—more freedom in your life.

Investing in Yourself

If you think about your life in terms of mental and emotional real estate, you will find it easier to shift your perspective to one of "investing" rather than "coping with" or "managing" your life. This means that every time you take action and make the choice to heal your Karma, it is like making a deposit in your well-being account.

When life becomes about investing in yourself for your overall benefit, it gets easier to make choices that are aligned with healing your Karma. In addition to healing your Karma, the choices you make that result in more freedom can also serve to create good Karma for your future. This is the ultimate goal and journey of the soul, to be free of Karma and return to oneness.

Healing Karma With Invocations

"Healing is a daily event. You can't 'go somewhere' to be healed; you must go inward to be healed."

– Dr. Nicole LePera

What are invocations? A good way to think of an invocation is that it's something you say to call on help from a supernatural force to create some sort of outcome. You can state an invocation aloud or in your head, though it's generally considered to be more powerful if spoken. The "supernatural force" can be whatever is part of your preferred belief system or practice.

Around the world, many different types of invocations are used for different purposes, including healing Karma. Even though there are many, there are three commonly known invocations that might be most effective: Prayers, Mantras, and Blessings. Though all three are a form of invocation, they differ in their context and the intent behind each will matter as much as the words themselves, if not more.

For example, blessings are most often other-focused in their alignment with another person, providing you with an opportunity to express compassion. Conversely, a mantra is typically self-focused and provides you with guidance and reminders on your path in ways that are both thoughtful and consistent. Meanwhile, prayers can be both self- and other-focused.

How you use each of these interventions is up to you. Therefore, in order to choose what's best for your particular karmic situation, it would be helpful to learn more about each of them and how they can help you heal your Karma and progress in your soul's journey.

Prayers

Though prayer is most often associated with religion, it doesn't have to be. Prayer is, in its simplest form, an expression of a desire

Examples of Prayers to Heal Karma

"Dear God, Please use me as a vessel of hope and healing for myself and others in this lifetime. Allow me to be an example for others in how to live a life in alignment with the highest good, for all. Thank you."

"Dear God, Thank you for allowing me to be of service to my world and community in ways that are benevolent to all who are in need. Give me eyes to see suffering and tools to help remedy it. Grant me patience and strength to be present and to choose a path that is for the greatest good. Amen."

"Dear God, Thank you for the many blessings in my life, and for the continued blessings I receive. Thank you for helping me be a blessing to others just as I have received blessings. Amen."

"Dear God, I pray for the guidance and insight to focus my energy where it is most needed and to be a beacon of hope and a source of inspiration and help for others. Thank you for this life. Amen."

"Dear God, Please help me to find forgiveness for the wrongs I have done to others and the strength to atone for what I have said or done. I ask for your help for those I have hurt and request your guidance in allowing me to create a life aligned with the greater good. Thank you."

Add your own prayer here:

or a hope. Nothing more and nothing less. This simplicity does not in any way diminish the power of prayer or its significance; it can be a very powerful force and energy.

In general, there are three main types of prayer: Connection, Gratitude, and Intercession. Though different, all three invoke something outside ourselves in their focus, such as a deity. For ease of communication in this book, we will refer to "God" as that deity and use "Amen" to signify the end of a prayer, which roughly translates to "so be it." [10] All three types of prayer use some form of focus (deity) and closure, though they differ in their intent.

A **prayer of Connection** is like sending a text or a love letter to God. It asks for nothing more than to be connected. A **prayer of Gratitude** is similar, but it adds a layer to the message. It includes an expression of appreciation for something (presumably given or supported by God). Both are simpler than the prayer of Intercession, which is more akin to an invocation in its intent, since it's asking for help.

A **prayer of Intercession** is a plea; it's a request to intervene, usually on behalf of someone else. It also carries a specific focus underneath the plea. These are the prayers that one hears most often in crisis—when there is tragedy, loss, trauma, or fear. Prayers of Intercession can also carry some sense of urgency to them. As such, they are less about connection and gratitude and more about desperation and need.

When it comes to healing Karma, it is probably best to start with prayers of Connection and Gratitude. This approach will help ease you into understanding how prayer can work as an invocation to help you create the new perspective and shift you seek.

Mantras

There is a simple truth in the universe that what you focus on will eventually appear. Time is the active variable. A mantra serves to help you focus. When you focus your energy, as well as your actions and behaviors, you can create significant change in your life. This is how you heal your Karma.

---

[10] Please use whatever name and closing word you prefer.

Examples of Mantras to Heal Karma

"I am a being of Light, and I choose to bring forth peace, harmony, and hope."

"I choose to participate in my life from a place of hope, joy, love, and alignment with all good things. Today and everyday."

"My life is a blessing to myself and others. I am aligned with joy, purpose, hope, and possibility."

"I am resilient, smart, and kind. I choose to align with that which I am at my core and know peace."

"I am human and may make mistakes; I commit to righting the wrongs I have made as quickly as possible, and to move forward with peace knowing I have done my best."

"Living a good life is a choice I get to make today, and every day."

"Kindness is my fuel."

Add your own mantra here:

A mantra is a consistent or daily message you are sending to your mind, body, and soul. Often received subliminally, it can serve as a reminder to realign with something you have identified as important. As such, mantras are predominantly used as tools. When it comes to healing Karma, mantras can be incredibly powerful interventions.

By committing to changing for the better, you are deliberately healing the Karma that you have collected in your life, or lifetimes. Some examples of what this can look like include: being kinder to others (including yourself), doing service work, approaching your day with peace in your heart, managing your anger and reactivity, and so much more!

Mantras can help you do all of this by providing a tangible reminder of the commitments you have made to yourself and your future. You heal your Karma when you raise your awareness to the changes you wish to make and embody those choices.

Blessings

When you offer someone a blessing, you are living in a space of high compassion. This alignment with your higher self can only lead to more calm, inner peace, and well-being. This is a powerful way to heal your Karma.

Of course, it goes without saying that the intention behind the blessing matters. You cannot offer a blessing without meaning it and expect for it to do good. The blessing must be genuine and authentic, and when it is, incredible things can happen.

People often confuse blessings with prayers, though they are significantly different. The main difference between a blessing and a prayer is that a prayer maintains some measure of attachment to an outcome, whereas a blessing does not.

When you offer someone a blessing, it is like making an anonymous donation. Though you may want to know about the outcome, you are not attached to it. Blessings are the gift you give away. Thankfully, they are infinite. There is no limit to how many blessings you can offer. What matters is that you are authentic in your offering.

A blessing, therefore, is one of the most altruistic actions you can take in healing your Karma and positively impacting your future.

How you choose to work on your Karma is up to you. Guidance from professionals can help you engage with healing in new ways, but blessings, mantras, and prayers are one of the easiest places to start.

Examples of Blessings to Heal Karma

"May you find peace in your heart and healing in your journey."

"Bless this person and all who know them that they may know kindness and love."

"May they heal from within and know the peace that comes from unconditional love, joy, and hope."

"May we all choose a path aligned with community, hope, healing, and the love that comes from living in harmony with respect and understanding. May the earth be at peace."

"May all beings be granted the Light of love and hope. May they heal and know joy."

Add your own blessing here:

Meditation to Heal Karma

"Meditation is the dissolution of thoughts in eternal awareness or pure consciousness without objectification, knowing without thinking, merging finitude in infinity."

– Voltaire

In addition to invocations, there are other ways to help heal your Karma and positively influence your future, including meditation.

Meditation has been around for thousands of years, with the earliest evidence of written records presumed to be the ancient Indian Vedas (c. 1500 BCE). This implies that humans have had a need to go quietly inward for as long as we can remember, and definitely throughout all of the modern era.

Meditation, as a practice, is about presence more than anything else. This is why it is helpful in healing Karma. There are many different forms of meditation, from more formal practices to the simple act of being present while sipping a cup of tea. By being present, you are neither focusing on the past nor are you fixating on the future; you are in the here and now. By being present, you can best assess where you would like to make changes for the better.

As you now know, awareness is one of the first steps toward changing and healing your Karma. Being present is a requirement of awareness. Engaging in a daily practice brings your mind and body into harmony and helps you create a clearer perspective. This will allow you to make more aligned decisions as you move forward in life, thereby healing your Karma.

Types of Meditation

Meditation can be both taught and learned. As such, it is important to figure out what works best for you and your situation. There are many types of meditation, but the two most common are:

1. Daily (learned) practice of quieting the mind, such as Transcendental Meditation, breath work, or others

2. Guided meditations from trusted sources, either in-person, or recorded

Daily Practice

To find the best daily practice for you, consider:

- Your environment
- Your time allowance
- Your commitment

It takes time to create a consistent practice, as well as a bit of trial and error. Be patient and the right model will show up. Also, do not overdo it or overthink it. Your practice does not need to start with an hour of silence, or even 20 minutes of sitting quietly in a yoga position. Your practice can start—and *should* start—with what you are able to do consistently. If this is ten minutes of coloring[11] or two minutes of focused breathing, that's what it is. Don't judge your practice; flow with it. What works is what's best.

Guided Meditation

To find the best guided meditation for you, consider:

- Trusted resources
- Purpose of the meditation
- Your personal limitations and resources

Building a good repertoire of guided meditations should take your personal situation and preferences into account. There are

---

[11] Coloring can be a great form of meditation, as I shared in an article I wrote years ago, including how I was originally inspired by Ozzy Osbourne to take up coloring. Go to the Resources section for an easy link.

numerous free sources for guided meditations online, just as there are an incredible amount of paid options. When considering guided meditations, I have found that what matters most to me is the tone of voice. If it's a voice I cannot listen to, I have lost before I begin. Not every voice is good for everyone, and not every voice suits the purpose or intent of your meditation.

If, for example, you want a meditation to help you sleep, you will want a voice that lulls you into deep rest. However, you would not want the same voice for a 5-minute meditation you do in the middle of a busy day to calm your mind at work. Experiment with different voices and resources to find what works best for you, and be open to having it change over time.

A Note About Guided Meditations

In the current era, where Artificial Intelligence (AI) is being used more and more frequently without any clear notification, it is increasingly important to do your due diligence. When we use guided meditations, we are taking a journey with another person (or soul) as our guide. In essence, we are opening ourselves up to others, and if you do not know the source of the guidance, it has the potential to be problematic.

Always vet any guided meditation before using it by reading a transcript. Make sure it is aligned with your values, beliefs, and goals, and then check sources. Though guided meditation is not the same as hypnosis, it is a close relative. In fact, it's probably more akin to being a half-sibling than a third cousin twice removed.

Do your homework and choose a professional whose work makes you feel lighter and more connected in your heart. This is always a good measurement of whether something is in alignment.

A Guided Meditation for Healing Karma

One of the things you can do if resources are limited is to record your own guided meditation. To do so, you need only create a voice recording of a script you have written or someone has given you. This does not need to be high-tech, nor should it be. This is for your own personal use, not anybody else's. To assist you with this, I have crafted a guided meditation specifically for healing Karma. You can record yourself reading it and then listen to it whenever you have time as part of your healing journey.[12] (You can also access this recording via the link on the Resources page of this book.)

~~~~~~

Let's start with making sure you are comfortable. Whether you are sitting or lying down, see if you can feel your body connect with the surface beneath you. Feel the floor or the cushions against your skin. Feel yourself settle into this space, and as you settle, start with your breath. Take three slow, clearing breaths. With each breath, I invite you to feel your body soften into the surface beneath you. As you inhale, your muscles lift slightly, and then exhale and feel yourself drop further into a comfortable and relaxed space. Breathe in... and breathe out. One more time: breathe in... breathe out. Now, take a moment to just be in this space, allowing your body to breathe for itself.

As you feel yourself connected to the place where you are, envision yourself moving into a place that is beautiful, whatever that means for you. It's a gentle place, filled with softness and light. As you move into it, you hear something in the distance, like the sound of gently falling water. Using your breath, allow yourself to move toward the sound until you see a lovely small fountain in front of you. This is the fountain of clearing. Its waters hold healing properties, and it invites you to come closer.

---

[12] Recording tip: Speak slowly.

Around the fountain, everything is shimmering, like gold and light at the same time. You are drawn to the peace you feel as you look at it, and you use your breath to move closer to the fountain's edge. As you stand directly in front of it, you can see your reflection in the water. It's a reflection of you at your happiest, calmest, and most joy-filled and peaceful. You smile as you see yourself in the water.

Now, as you lean forward, reach your right hand into the water and place your left hand on your heart. Watch as you allow the golden light from the water move up into your hand and across your chest to your heart. Let the healing waters infuse your body with golden light, as you hold your heart, continually breathing in peace, healing, and joy.

Allow your body to release any fragments of completed Karma that it has been holding onto through the soles of your feet. Mother Earth will willingly take it and use it as raw energy to create something beautiful, something new. Releasing to the earth is a gift. Allow the golden light water to move throughout your body. If you feel it get stuck anywhere, use your breath to continue to move it on. Your breath can be a vessel for the healing waters.

When you feel that your whole body is filled with the golden light, lift your eyes to the space above you and see that all is good. Turn back to the fountain of water, with gratitude, and thank the waters for bringing you on this journey of healing. Bow your head in appreciation, as you pull your right hand out of the waters and let your left hand slowly fall away from your chest.

With your hands relaxed by your side, breathe deeply and feel your body and divine soul radiating with golden light. Breathe again and thank yourself for taking this step toward healing and love. And with your third breath, allow yourself to begin to come back to the present moment. The fountain will slowly move away from you now, and you will begin to feel the edges of your body again. You can feel the connection to the surface beneath you as you use your breath to wake your cells to the here and now.

You may wish to wiggle your toes and your fingers, your nose and your mouth. Move your shoulders up and down, as you breathe in again. Back in the space that you are in, allow your eyes to regain their sight as you take in your surroundings. Move your limbs and your torso to come fully back into your body, and take a deep clearing breath bringing yourself back to full consciousness. Pause for a moment, bringing your hands together in front of your heart, to say thank you to yourself for choosing to heal, then thanking the earth and the waters for helping you clear and heal your Karma.
With gratitude.

Life by Design or Default

"If your actions were to boomerang back on you instant-ly, would you still act the same?"

– Alexandra Katehakis

At the end of the day, Karma may be a Universal Law, but it is also a compass through which you can guide your life. It is, in that sense, like a roadmap to a journey you have not yet taken, but one that has all the best landmarks (and detours) already listed. In other words, it's the tool by which you can create your best life imaginable—both in this lifetime and the next.

How do you create this guide? It all boils down to choice: You can either live your life deliberately or by default.

Living By Default

The person who lives life by default is the one who often finds themself being more reactionary than not. They perhaps always feel like a victim, or like life is happening *to* them. Living by default is what happens when we allow external forces and our environment (people, situations, etc.) to make our decisions for us. This can build resentment, anger, and frustration—which can lead to us wanting to wish harm on someone, because we can't see a way out of the pain.

When we feel backed into a corner, we sometimes develop a need to fight our way out by harming those we either blame for our position or who we feel are in our way, without realizing that it's not usually a corner we are in and that there may be another way out. If you find yourself blaming someone else for your circumstances and life, it's important to truly look at what deci-sions *you* could have made differently before placing blame. This is the way of Karma: Taking ownership for your life and behaving accordingly.

Of course, there are times when someone else's actions have resulted in the situation you are in. While Karma is probably at play on a soul level, the choice in this lifetime still remains: To wish harm, or not.

Ultimately, wishing harm is never a good decision because… Karma. Instead, there is a better way: Living deliberately.

Living Deliberately

Living deliberately is about raising your awareness to your life in such a way that you begin to feel the most empowered. In other words, you get to choose—and are choosing—how you show up, who you are in relationship with, and how you are interacting with people and situations in your life.

This is not selfish; this is about knowing yourself and having good boundaries. It's also about not taking on someone else's Karma. Though it may feel difficult at first because you're not used to it, the more you practice living deliberately, the easier it becomes.

If, for example, you already feel backed into a corner, it will take some patience and a dedication to being consistent in your choices to create a different way. Mantras can help with this. They serve as daily reminders for what you actually want—what you are actually choosing—which is a life with freedom at its core.

Healing Karma (and creating good Karma) is easier when you choose to live your life deliberately. The best news is that it's a choice you can make every day.

Conclusion

"There is a wonderful mythical law of nature that the three things we crave most in life—happiness, freedom, and peace of mind—are always attained by giving them to someone else."

– Peyton Conway March

Understanding Karma is about understanding yourself—what drives you, what you are feeling, who you are, what you want and why. When you take the time to connect with your inner being in a direct and compassionate way, you empower yourself to make different choices. These choices can lead to healing, forgiveness, and freedom, which all leads to better Karma for both the present and the future.

Focusing on your Karma is one of the best gifts you can give yourself and the world. As you heal, you also remove opportunities and the desire to hurt or harm others. Harming others is never a good idea and rarely results in positive results. Choosing to heal yourself, instead of harming others, creates more harmony in your life, which can only be of benefit. Ultimately, though healing Karma starts with you, it can have positive ripple effects throughout the world. Thankfully.

May you find the courage, peace, and joy you seek as you journey toward understanding—and healing—your Karma.

Appendix

To follow is the original blog that inspired Understanding Karma and resulted in the series and this book. *[Originally published 13 August 2018 on Inspirebytes.com by Martina E. Faulkner, MSW[13]]*

Original Blog: *The Law of Karma and Wishing Harm on Others*

When is it ok to wish ill on someone?

Well, the short answer is: never.

And the long answer is: Really, NEVER.

It's never ok to wish harm on anyone else. If you do, you're actually inviting that bad energy back into your life tenfold. Karma doesn't discriminate in that regard – what you reap, you will (eventually) sow. Always.

I actually know of several "spiritual" teachers who have given clients invocations of harm toward another person. Every time I hear of it – I shudder. (Seriously, yikes!) Thankfully, my first brush with understanding this simple truth came from my Reiki grandfather who taught me a very simple lesson: You never impose your will on anyone else. Ever. To do so is to practice black magic, and it will always rebound onto you. Always.

I learned this within the first week of studying Reiki and beginning to uncover my own gifts, but millennia of history in other traditions teach the same message, most commonly:

Do unto others as you would have them do unto you.

If you don't want someone wishing harm on you, don't wish it on others. It's really that simple. We only choose to make it more complicated by employing the three most dysfunctional attributes of the mind: justification, generalization, and rationalization.

---

[13] The original blog with some comments and responses remains on inspirebytes.com.

Perhaps, though, rather than getting mired in the teachings of the past, or the simple truths that echo through their wisdom, it might be more practical today to think of it this way:

You can't cast a negative net and expect to catch anything positive.

Nothing good comes from sowing or spewing venom or toxicity in the world. Even though it might "feel" good in the moment, it will ultimately cause more problems in the long run. Of course, the long run could be your next lifetime, but that still doesn't make it right.

In this age of instant gratification and guarded consequences, it's increasingly more important for us to remember the simple truths and the wisdom of the ages. They've lasted as long as they have because they're as pure as it gets. Time can't tarnish them.

As for what to do when you feel wronged by someone? It's 100% natural to vent, cry, get angry and experience all of the emotions running through your body… stopping just short of desiring harm on the other party. Not only will you be properly managing your Karma, you'll also actually feel better for not having created more toxicity in the situation. That's a win-win if ever there was one.

Or, as another great teacher once taught: turn the other cheek. Which can either translate as 1) allow yourself to be hit again, or 2) (as I prefer) turn and walk away, removing yourself from the drama of the other person, and staying true to who you are.

There's no shame in disengaging. The only real loss is when you choose to engage in something destructive and negative from a place of hurt or fear, because it perpetuates the cycle of harm – a cycle you're standing squarely in the middle of. Yikes!

Discussion Guide

Over the years, I have found that understanding and application need to go hand in hand when creating change. This prompted me to ask: How can I help someone more easily apply what they've learned in this book? The answer was to provide a tangible starting point through a Discussion Guide.

Each topic in this book was chosen specifically to encourage thought, reflection, and discussion. Every word was written to help you develop a deeper understanding of common issues, which can then support and empower you to create positive change in your life. Below, you will find thoughtful questions for each topic as well as for the book as a whole. They can be used privately as prompts for journaling, or they can be used by groups (book clubs, process groups, etc.) to inspire conversation and new ways of thinking and relating.

My hope is that this Discussion Guide will invite you to go deeper and explore your own beliefs, thoughts, and ideas about these foundational aspects of life, prompting you to make choices that are aligned with your best self. In short, I hope that you will find possibility in these pages—the possibility of a happier, more loving, and more peaceful life through understanding.

~~~~~

Discussion Questions for UNDERSTANDING

Understanding is a word that is often, ironically, misunderstood. When we think we understand something, we don't always, and too often we are afraid or too shy to admit it. So, let's start with what it means to "understand" something or someone.

1. What does "understanding" mean to you?

2. Take a moment to complete these sentences:

    a. "I think people feel most understood when…"

b. "I feel understood when…"

c. "When I feel misunderstood, I tend to…"

d. "When I don't understand someone or something, I tend to…"

3. Now, fill in the blank: One area of my life where I would like to have a deeper understanding is _____ .

When it comes to understanding, we need to be active participants in how we show up, including a willingness to ask questions. This is true whether we are trying to understand another person's perspective or gain a deeper understanding of a particular topic or issue for ourselves. The six topics in this book (Resilience, Grief, Compassion, Energy, Gratitude, and Karma) were all written to provide a basic understanding of what it can mean to be human. So, let's start with the larger context and then move into each topic, specifically.

1. What is your primary takeaway from the book, as a whole? Try writing it in one sentence.

2. What are common themes among all the topics? How do these show up in your life?

3. Of the six topics or the common themes, which one do you want or need to focus on the most right now in your life? Why?

4. How can developing a new understanding of this issue help you?

5. What next steps can you take to both create and apply a new understanding in your life?

Discussion Questions for Resilience

1. When was a time in your life when you felt most resilient? When did you feel least resilient?

2. What is one area of your life where you could do due diligence and build up your resilience?

3. Since resilience is a byproduct of other things, what can you engage in to help build more resilience in your daily life?

4. Do you tend to feel more powerful or more empowered? How can you work to feel more empowered in your daily life?

5. Are you holding on to any negative memories? How can you make the shift from holding them to remembering them?

Discussion Questions for Grief

1. What new information did you learn about grief? How can you use this information to support you or someone you care about?

2. If you have cultural, religious, or personal rituals for mourning, what are they? How do they differ for loss through death vs. other types of loss?

3. Think about your personal experiences. With your new understanding of the types of loss, do any of those experiences fall under one of the categories of grief that you hadn't previously realized, such as regret?

4. What resources do you have for when you experience grief? What new resources can you find that work for you?

5. How can you be with someone who is currently grieving? How would you want someone to show up for you?

Discussion Questions for Compassion

1. How do you define compassion?

2. How would you define the role of a caregiver as you have experienced or witnessed it in your life? What would you change, if you could?

3. When was the last time you took perspective and really made an effort to understand someone else's position or experience? What was the result?

4. Thinking of a time when you experienced empathy from someone, list three things that you felt as a result. How did their empathy change your experience?

5. Compassion is greater than the sum of its parts. How has compassion showed up in your life?

Discussion Questions for Energy

1. Think about the energy in the room around you. What does it feel like? How would you describe it from both a feeling and physical perspective?

2. Remember a time when you noticed the energy around you shift dramatically. Now, identify the reason for the change. How did it affect you, and how can you respond differently in the future if it happens again?

3. How and where can you start setting emotional boundaries in order to protect your energy?

4. We are all responsible for the energy frequency we bring to our environments. What do you most want to change about how you show up in various situations, such as: family gatherings, work events, entertainment or social outings? How can you interact differently?

5. What is one thing you want to learn more about with regard to energy? What steps can you take to start that process?

Discussion Questions for Gratitude

1. Have you experienced performative gratitude? If so, how did it make you feel? If not, how could you respond if it happens in the future?

2. Are there times in your life when you feel your gratitude is on autopilot, instead of embodying it? What's the main difference for you?

3. When you don't feel like being grateful, how do you show up? How can you shift into a place of gratitude?

4. If you have one, how has a gratitude practice impacted your life? If you don't have one, how would you like to create one?

5. Gratitude takes us from our head to our heart, almost instantly. Understanding that lower frequency emotions tend to reside in our head and higher frequency emotions tend to reside in our heart, what is the balance between your head and your heart on a daily basis?

Discussion Questions for Karma

1. As the different groups are described, how would you define your own Soul Pod, Soul Family, and Soul Mirror? Who in your life is in each group and why?

2. What does Reason/Season/Lifetime mean to you? Make a list of people in your life in all three categories. What is the interplay between these groups, for you?

3. If you recently wished ill on someone, how do you plan to reverse the Karma from that?

4. Which type of invocation do you need most right now, prayers, mantras, or blessings? Write down a few of your own using the examples in the book as a guide.

5. Are you living by default or living deliberately? What choices can you make to be more intentional in your life and how you interact with the world around you?

Resources

To follow are various resources you might find helpful as you begin working with your new sense of understanding for the different topics covered in this book.

A Guided Meditation for Healing Karma

To support you on your journey and make it easier for you, I recorded the guided meditation I shared in this book. Coupled with beautiful ambient music, it is designed to help you create a path to healing your Karma and living a more balanced and peace-filled life.

"Daily Dose of Gratitude" Page

This FREE and downloadable PDF is a single page that you can print to start your journey with gratitude in an easy and meaningful way.

Blog on Coloring and Ozzy Osbourne

It's over a decade later, and I still use coloring as a form of meditation. Thanks, Ozzy! (RIP)

UNDERSTANDING Podcast Links

Dr. Kate Lund and I sat down to discuss each of the six topics in greater depth on her podcast *The Optimized Mind*. During our conversations, we discussed real-life examples and some of the more nuanced aspects of each subject. You can find her podcast on all the major platforms, including: Spotify, Apple, and Amazon. QR Codes for each episode on Apple are listed below:

Resilience   Energy

Grief   Gratitude

Compassion   Karma

At the end of the series, we also recorded a longer podcast covering this book and discussed more of my thoughts behind the scenes. It will be released in conjunction with the book, so head to *The Optimized Mind* to give it a listen.

Quotes

My whole life, I have loved and collected quotes. I find comfort, inspiration, and validation in reading others' words, especially when I feel that they perfectly capture something I am feeling or trying to understand. As such, I used quotes deliberately throughout the standalone books as an intentional part of the design. For this book, however, that didn't make sense as it would detract from the reading experience.

Instead, I used many of them at the start of each section and have included the rest below. This way, they remain a part of this work, and hopefully they will serve to inspire you in whatever way you need.

Quotes on Resilience

"Fear has been given a bad rep. It isn't something to be avoided; rather, it is our life's mission. It's our duty to overcome our fears, whatever they may be. ... It is up to us to accept our own powers and make up our own minds, and not leave it to someone else." – Levison Wood

"Out of suffering have emerged the strongest souls; the most massive characters are seared with scars." – Khalil Gibran

"It is really wonderful how much resilience there is in human nature. Let any obstructing cause, no matter what, be removed in any way, even by death, and we fly back to the first principles of hope and enjoyment." – Bram Stoker

"A good half of the art of living is resilience." – Alain de Botton

"My scars remind me that I did indeed survive my deepest wounds. That in itself is an accomplishment. And they bring to mind something else, too. They remind me that the damage life has inflicted on me has, in many places, left me stronger and more resilient. What hurt me in the past has actually made me better equipped to face the present." – Steve Goodier

"The human capacity for burden is like bamboo—far more flexible than you'd ever believe at first glance." – Jodi Picoult

"Although the world is full of suffering, it is also full of the overcoming of it."
– Helen Keller

"Our greatest glory is not in never falling, but in rising every time we fall."
– Confucius

"No matter how bleak or menacing a situation may appear, it does not entirely own us. It can't take away our freedom to respond, our power to take action."
– Ryder Carroll

"If your heart is broken, make art with the pieces." – Shane Koyczan

"Forgive yourself for your faults and your mistakes and move on." – Les Brown

"No matter how much falls on us, we keep plowing ahead. That's the only way to keep the roads clear." – Greg Kincaid

"Enthusiasm is common. Endurance is rare." – Angela Duckworth

"I knew exactly what kind of effort I was going to need to get where I wanted to go." – Vernon Davis

"Resilience is very different than being numb. Resilience means you experience, you feel, you fail, you hurt. You fall. But, you keep going."
– Yasmini Mogahed

"No one escapes pain, fear, and suffering. Yet from pain can come wisdom, from fear can come courage, from suffering can come strength—if we have the virtue of resilience." – Eric Greitens

Quotes on Grief

"Your memory feels like home to me. So whenever my mind wanders, it always finds its way back to you." – Ranata Suzuki

"The friend who can be silent with us in a moment of despair or confusion, who can stay with us in an hour of grief and bereavement, who can tolerate not knowing... not healing, not curing... that is a friend who cares." – Henri Nouwen

"Sometimes, only one person is missing, and the whole world seems depopulated."
– Alphonse de Lamartine

"Look closely and you will see almost everyone carrying bags of cement on their shoulders. That's why it takes courage to get out of bed in the morning and climb into the day." – Edward Hirsch

"Anything that's human is mentionable, and anything that is mentionable, can be more manageable. When we can talk about our feelings, they become less overwhelming, less upsetting, and less scary. The people we trust with that important talk can help us know that we are not alone." – Fred Rogers

"There is no grief like the grief that does not speak." – Henry Wadsworth

"Everyone must leave something behind when he dies, my grandfather said. A child or a book or a painting or a house or a wall built or a pair of shoes made. Or a garden planted. Something your hand touches some way so your soul has somewhere to go when you die, and when people look at that tree or that flower you planted, you're there." – Ray Bradbury, Fahrenheit 451

Quotes on Compassion

"Our human compassion binds us the one to the other - not in pity or patronizingly, but as human beings who have learnt how to turn our common suffering into hope for the future." – Nelson Mandela

"The dew of compassion is a tear." – Lord Byron

"In order to have Understanding, you need forgiveness, compassion, and empathy."– Rooney Mara

"Compassion will cure more sins than condemnation." – Henry Ward Beecher

"It is above all by the imagination that we achieve perception and compassion and hope." – Ursula K. Le Guin

"Compassion is not a virtue—it is a commitment. It's not something we have or don't have—it's something we choose to practice." – Brené Brown

"My mission in life is not merely to survive, but to thrive; and to do so with some passion, some compassion, some humor, and some style." – Maya Angelou

"Those who are truly strong can afford to show compassion." – Patrik Baboumian

"Compassion is the keen awareness of the interdependence of all things."
– Thomas Merton

"I learned compassion from being discriminated against. Everything bad that's ever happened to me has taught me compassion." – Ellen DeGeneres

"Compassion for others begins with kindness to ourselves." – Pema Chödrön

"Everyone deserves compassion." – Michael Sheen

"We rise by lifting others." – Robert Ingersoll

"As the human race, let's continue to show love, compassion, and respect towards one another." – Amber Liu

Quotes on Energy

"Love the moment and the energy of that moment will spread beyond all boundaries." – Corita Kent

"Don't hold on to anger, hurt, or pain. They steal your energy and keep you from love." – Leo Buscaglia

"The energy of the mind is the essence of life." – Aristotle

"The way you think, the way you behave, the way you eat, can influence your life by 30 to 50 years." – Deepak Chopra

"I do believe we're all connected. I do believe in positive energy. I do believe in the power of prayer. I do believe in putting good out into the world. And I believe in taking care of each other." – Harvey Fierstein

"Love is a sacred reserve of energy; it is like the blood of spiritual evolution."
– Pierre Teilhard de Chardin

"Love is an energy which exists of itself. It is its own value." – Thornton Wilder

"What drains your spirit drains your body. What fuels your spirit fuels your body." – Caroline Myss

"The body's energy flow, like a river, must be kept clear to avoid stagnation and disease." – Donna Eden

"Positive energy knows no boundaries. If everyone were to spread positive energy on the Internet, the world would be a much better place." – Lu Wei

"There is a vitality, a life force, an energy, a quickening, that is translated through you into action, and because there is only one of you in all time, this expression is unique." – Martha Graham

"Thoughts are mental energy; they're the currency that you have to attract what you desire. Learn to stop spending that currency on thoughts you don't want." – Wayne Dyer, PhD

"Between stimulus and response, there is a space. In that space is our power to choose our response. In our response lies our growth and our freedom." – Victor Frankl

"It takes as much energy to wish as it does to plan." – Eleanor Roosevelt

"Thought is pure energy, every thought you have, have ever had, and ever will have is creative. The energy of your thought never dies. It leaves your being and heads out into the universe, extending forever." – Neale Donald Walsh

"When you are enthusiastic about what you do, you feel this positive energy. It's very simple." – Paulo Coelho

"The more you lose yourself in something bigger than yourself, the more energy you will have." – Norman Vincent Peale

Quotes on Gratitude

"Gratitude is a virtue annexed to justice, because it is concerned with rendering to someone what is due to him on account of a benefit received." – Thomas Aquinas

"We should try by all means to be as grateful as possible. For gratitude is a good thing for ourselves, in a sense in which justice, that is commonly supposed to concern other persons, is not; gratitude returns in large measure unto itself." – Seneca

"Gratitude can transform any situation. It alters your vibration, moving you from negative energy to positive. It's the quickest, easiest, most powerful way to effect change in your life." – Oprah

"Something so simple, but it's important to take the time out from living and just appreciate what you've got right in front of you." – L.A. Fiore

"Silent gratitude isn't much use to anyone." – G.B. Stern

"Showing gratitude is one of the simplest yet most powerful things humans can do for each other." – Randy Pausch

"A grateful mind is a great mind which eventually attracts to itself great things." – Plato

"When we give cheerfully and accept gratefully, everyone is blessed." – Maya Angelou

"Gratitude is the memory of the heart." – Jean Baptiste Massieu

"She could go on asking herself why roses had thorns or she could be thankful that thorns had roses." – Ella Griffin

"Acknowledging the good that you already have in your life is the foundation for all abundance." – Eckhart Tolle

"Gratitude is not only the greatest of virtues, but the parent of all others." – Cicero

Quotes on Karma

"Don't judge each day by the harvest you reap but by the seeds that you plant." – Robert Louis Stevenson

"Like gravity, karma is so basic we often don't even notice it." – Sakyong Mipham

"Realize that everything connects to everything else." – Leonardo da Vinci

"I believe in karma, and I believe if you put out positive vibes to everybody, that's all you're going to get back." – Kesha

"The ones you judge today may be the judgments you endure tomorrow." – Unknown

"When you see a good person, think of becoming like her/him. When you see someone not so good, reflect on your own weak points." – Confucius

"What you hate, you re-create; and what you bless, you put to rest." – *Eric Micha'el Leventhal*

"When you truly understand karma, then you realize you are responsible for everything in your life." – *Keanu Reeves*

"Live a good and honorable life. Then, when you are older, you can look back and enjoy it a second time." – *Dalai Lama*

"It is better in prayer to have a heart without words than words without heart." – *Mahatma Gandhi*

"A mantra is a powerful tool to quiet the mind and focus your intention." – *Unknown*

"You never know where a blessing can come from." – *Teena Marie*

"Karma is not just about the troubles, but also about surmounting them." – *Rick Springfield*

Acknowledgments

Though writing is often fairly solitary, creating a book is never a solo endeavor. This book and the series came together with thoughtful input and assistance from others, especially Franny and Katherine. Thank you both for being integral to the entire process—from conception to the final work. Your feedback and support made everything easier. To Dan for your valuable perspective as a group facilitator and help in creating the Discussion Guide. To my design team at One-to-One for always being supportive of my vision. To my mom and friends for championing each standalone book as they came out; as always, I truly appreciate your support. And to Dr. Kate Lund for your kind and thoughtful words in the Foreword and for taking the time to speak with me about each topic on your podcast, *The Optimized Mind*. I really enjoyed our discussions as well as having the opportunity to focus on each subject in more detail.

Finally, thank you to you, my readers, especially those that have been with me since the very beginning. This book feels like a return to my writing roots. It's because of you that I continue to find inspiration and ideas to write about to help others on this journey that we call life.

Thank you.

About the Author

"The quality of your life is based on the choices you make."
– Martina E. Faulkner

Martina E. Faulkner is a cross-genre author, speaker, and thought leader whose work explores what it means to be human—what makes us both unique and universal. With a distinctive background in mental health and healing—as a therapist, certified life coach, and Reiki Master Teacher—Martina is a modern-day Mystic who brings a truly rare perspective to her writing, whether fiction, non-fiction, poetry, or children's books. Beyond her passion for sharing ideas, Martina is a daily tea drinker, loves dogs, and has never met an Oxford comma she didn't like!

You can read Martina's weekly column *Unique and Universal* on Substack, sign up for her monthly newsletter on her website, and follow Martina on social media (@martinaefaulkner). Visit martinafaulkner.com to learn more.

Other Books by Martina E. Faulkner

Love and Pain: Poetry From the Chambers of My Heart

What if..?: How to Create the Life You Want Using the Power of Possibility

50 and F*ck It!: Learn How You Can Let Go, Stand In Your Boots, and Truly Live!

Infinite In My Heart: Poems of Love, Loss, and Hope

Me: 365: A 5-Year Question-A-Day Journal

The Author's Journey: Your Roadmap to Navigating and Understanding the Publishing Industry

Crafting the Perfect College Essay: Write Your Best Essay in 3 Easy Steps

Children's Books by Tia Martina

Martina's debut children's book, *When the World Went Quiet*, chronicled true stories of nature resurfacing during the global pandemic of 2020. The book was gifted to Sir David Attenborough, who referred to it as "charming."

When the World Went Quiet

Princess Wigglebottom and the Forgotten Christmas

www.ingramcontent.com/pod-product-compliance
Lightning Source LLC
Chambersburg PA
CBHW030923120626
46554CB00001B/256

9 781969 348051